Praise for *I Didn't Do the Thing Today*

'A radical masterpiece, going against society's push for productivity and happiness, and instead calling for wholeness and integrity. Madeleine Dore provides us a wonderful blueprint for how to make our own days based on what delights, moves and inspires us. Whether you have your routine down to a science or you can't wake up early to save your life, this affirming book will have plenty of wise offerings, and a reminder that your way is the best way. While many books insist on changing your life, this one invites you to deepen and expand it.'

—Mari Andrew, author of *My Inner Sky*

'Deep, thoughtful, gently instructive, nourishing.'
—Clare Bowditch, author of *Your Own Kind of Girl*

'Madeleine Dore has done us a huge favour in reframing age-old wisdom and setting it in a very contemporary context. Read it and sigh with relief.'

—Hugh Mackay, author of *The Kindness Revolution*

'Incredibly relatable and perhaps more importantly, very necessary. A brilliant and timely book.'

—Julia Busuttil Nishimura, author of *Ostro*

D1471811

'Madeleine Dore may have originally set out to discover the one true secret of productivity, but the result of all her interviews and investigations is something vastly wiser and more useful than that. *I Didn't Do the Thing Today* is a remarkable combination: part broadside against our culture of frenetic busyness, part consolation for the days when things don't go to plan. It's also the best kind of productivity manual, filled with guidance for actually getting around to more of the things that matter.'

—Oliver Burkeman, author of *Four Thousand Weeks: Time Management for Mortals*

'*I Didn't Do the Thing Today* makes an important case for worrying less about getting things done and more about the things that are worth doing. I found a lot to steal here and you will, too.'

—Austin Kleon, author of *Steal Like an Artist*

I Didn't Do the Thing Today

I Didn't Do the Thing Today

On Letting Go of Productivity Guilt

Madeleine Dore

murdoch books
Sydney | London

Published in 2022 by Murdoch Books, an imprint of Allen & Unwin

Murdoch Books Australia
83 Alexander Street, Crows Nest NSW 2065
Phone: +61 (0)2 8425 0100
murdochbooks.com.au
info@murdochbooks.com.au

Murdoch Books UK
Ormond House, 26–27 Boswell Street, London WC1N 3JZ
Phone: +44 (0) 20 8785 5995
murdochbooks.co.uk
info@murdochbooks.co.uk

A catalogue record for this
book is available from the
National Library of Australia

ISBN 978 1 92235 150 0

Cover and text design by Evi O

Typeset by Midland Typesetters, Australia
Printed and bound in Great Britain by Clays Ltd, Elcograf S.p.A.

We acknowledge that we meet and work on the traditional lands of the Cammeraygal
people of the Eora Nation and pay our respects to their elders past, present and future.

10 9 8 7 6 5 4 3

Dedicated to the things that really matter,
which are rarely ever things,
but count for everything

Contents

I didn't do the thing today.
I didn't rise before seven. I didn't change.
I didn't pen lines of stream of consciousness.
I didn't take my time with a purposeful ritual.
I didn't diligently complete my tasks.
I didn't move stridently around the park.
I didn't write. I didn't start; I didn't finish.
I didn't achieve; I didn't progress.
And it didn't matter. For doing the thing today
Isn't the measure of a day.

The Thing About Advice

Perhaps it seems odd to open a book like this one, which explores topics such as productivity, balance and self-discipline, and discover that the author doesn't proclaim to have sorted out these things in life completely. I don't know the key to how to be better, to improve, to change, to fix. I don't think there is a secret hack, a right move to make that will cure the wobbly, messy, imperfect aspects of being human. Instead of changing these things about ourselves, I think they are the very things that are important to embrace as we manoeuvre through our days.

So rather than definitive advice, this book is the culmination of the lessons, thoughts, feelings, perspectives and insights I took from a project I started back in 2014 called *Extraordinary Routines*. It was a labour of love I began when I had just graduated from my degree and had no idea how to make a start—in my career in journalism, but also in building the kind of creative life I wanted. So I started speaking with friends about their days, and then to friends of friends, and ultimately to people I admired from afar whom I never dreamed I'd have the opportunity to speak with.

Without the funding, rigour or expertise of a formal research project, it was something I picked up and put down over the years as my time and curiosity allowed. I spoke with whom I could, when I could, where I could—mostly in my home city of Melbourne, but also in New York City when I visited. The project over the years became a place I went to explore questions and sort through my own bumps with things like productivity guilt, comparison and perfection, through conversations, experiments and my own musings.

And that's the place from which this book sets out. In many ways, it is the very definition of self-help: I wrote it to wonder aloud, to sort through the archive of conversations I had curated, to help myself through my own days, to help me see my own contradictions, mistakes, limitations, and to try to work with them as I came to understand myself better and find my own way. While some lessons can be generalised, what is presented here is me, the person I am, the people I was drawn to speaking to, the lessons I heard, the interpretations I made, the gaps I missed, the blind spots I had, the opinions I held at the time that might now have shifted. What might have inspired or motivated me, or provided meaning to me, may seem unworkable or even dull to you, because my perspective, my stumbles, my experiences will no doubt be different to yours. So by all means be discerning, pull the discussion apart, curate your own conversations. Take from this book what appeals to you, and put to the side what might not—and know that I'm figuring it out alongside you too.

And so with a gentle nudge, dear reader, I encourage you to explore what works for you and what doesn't, as you dip in and out of the chapters, to get up close to your own contradictions, your changing wants, your mistakes and limitations, and to give yourself the advice you need in this moment. And give yourself permission to change your own mind as your days change, too.

At the Start of the Day

1

The Narrowing of Productivity

We are great fools. 'He has passed his life in idleness,' say we:
'I have done nothing to-day.' What? have you not lived?
That is not only the fundamental, but the most
illustrious, of your occupations.

Michel de Montaigne, 'Of Experience'

There will be days like these. Days that aren't our day. Days we don't seize. Days when we wished to accomplish more. Days that blur in bitsy errands. Days that get derailed. Days when there is something we should be doing that we're not doing. Days when we worry about all that will be stacked onto tomorrow. Days when we're convinced everyone else is having a better day.

Such days can leave us feeling deflated. While I don't know the particular shape your days take, there are things we all stumble over as we try to navigate modern life. Whether you work nine-to-five in an office or you're a freelancer, a manager or a shift worker, or you might be a stay-at-home parent or a retiree, each of us is entangled in a culture that measures our value through productivity—how much we do, how well we do it, whom we do it for. For many of us, our days have become containers for internalised capitalism, or the pervading sense that what we do is tied to our worth.

When we conflate productivity with worthiness, what we do is never enough. We can always do more, and there is always more to do. There's the laundry thing, the catch-up thing, the replying to a text thing, the grocery shopping thing, the cooking thing, the cleaning thing, the creative thing, the exercise thing, the work thing, the medical thing, the thing we ought to do, the thing we don't want to do, the thing we've put off despite it being the one important thing.

With this pile of undone things often comes an undercurrent of guilt, anxiety or shame. Instead of being alive to the variances of what is done in a day—sometimes a little, sometimes a lot—we spiral in a slew of 'if onlys': if only I were more productive, if only I were more efficient, if only I were better, if only I were more like that person . . . then I could do it right, do enough, be enough.

So much of what we are trying to achieve in our days is bound to the idea that we can optimise things to the point of perfection. Surrounded by promises that if only we adopt this life hack or follow that morning routine we will finally get it all done, we look to this new thing to remedy our *days like these*. There can be a juicy pleasure in trying the latest hack, with its promise of improvement. I've made a hobby of it: I've eaten the frog, put butter in my morning coffee, bought the new planner, tried the miracle morning routine, set up rewards for good habits. These popular systems can be useful, and may even change your life, but I've found they can also create another thing to stumble over in our days.

When tomorrow arrives and we find that this new thing didn't fix us or we don't perfectly adhere to the system, we're right back at the beginning of the 'if only' spiral. Feeling like we're the only one who isn't getting it right, who keeps messing it up, we turn to the next thing in our hot pursuit of this better version of ourselves. We search again for a key to optimise our days, and stumble again, only to be met with self-blame.

We're running just to stand still, and we're missing the point. We're doing all this work to improve ourselves, only to go on judging ourselves for being imperfect. Yet such a pursuit is a fool's errand. The English word 'perfect' comes from the Latin verb *perficere*, which means 'to finish, complete, carry out or achieve'. When we pursue perfection in our days and in ourselves, we're creating an impossible standard. We've taken what's incomplete as proof there is something wrong with us, when in fact being imperfect is an inevitable part of being human. We blame ourselves for not being exactly where we think we should be. We berate ourselves for inactivity. We shrink in our self-comparison to others. We doubt our decisions. We become so stifled by the pressure of being productive that we sometimes don't do anything at all.

Rather than making us better, this 'doing obsession' leaves us feeling overwhelmed, burned out, dissatisfied, inadequate and alone. When others wear what they do as a badge of honour—talking in terms of busyness, of being flat out, of accolades and accomplishments—we feel inadequate by comparison, yet under pressure to do the same. Doing, doing, doing, all just to keep up, to prove we are worthwhile—yet we never quite feel that we get there.

In the swirl of it all, it's difficult to see that we're being set up to fail. We're told to work hard in a society that undervalues our labour. We're being told to self-optimise in a culture that also tells us we'll never be enough. Instead, we need to buy, pursue or do this thing if we're to have any hope of reaching contentment—all the while, we're chasing a shadow. If we aren't benefiting from our overwork, overdoing, overachieving, why do we insist on fastening our self-worth to how productive we are?

Perhaps we remain fixated on this optical illusion because this doing obsession can be easy to spot but difficult to resolve. In fact, it's seemingly impossible on our own to curtail productivity pressure and the subsequent anxiety, guilt or shame we experience. Even the countercalls to take a break, reduce stress or create self-care rituals become yet another thing to add to the to-do list.

As Cal Newport, who popularised the concept of 'deep work'— meaning the ability to focus on tasks without distraction—wrote in a *New Yorker* essay called 'The Rise and Fall of Getting Things Done', no tips, hacks or techniques directly address the fundamental problem: the insidiously haphazard way that work unfolds at the organisational level. We must, Newport says, 'acknowledge the futility of trying to tame our frenzied work lives all on our own, and instead ask, collectively, whether there's a better way to get things done'.

We may recognise that the pursuit of productivity is making us miserable, and yet have no idea how to fill our days instead. Even

I DIDN'T DO THE THING TODAY

as we live through the global health, social and climate crises of our time, many of us still feel bad for not doing enough or doing it right—and so pile another layer of guilt on ourselves.

For many of us, this has been amplified during the COVID-19 pandemic, amid the impacts and ripple effects it has had on our daily lives. For some, the change may have been minimal. For others, days have been emptied by job loss, crowded by additional pressures or hollowed out by grief. For some, it was the first time their days became their own to construct. No fixed start or finish times, no boss or team to be accountable to in person. For many of us, without the doing, we felt adrift.

The pandemic shook up our days in varying ways, but one thing it taught many of us is that we are always more adrift than we think. In our obsession with doing, we can overlook that life has a way of intervening in our plans for a productive day: distractions come to the fore, things fall through, responsibilities arise unexpectedly, and our minds and bodies don't always cooperate with our expectations.

When we don't meet the high standard of productivity we set for ourselves, we feel bad—overlooking the fact that the benchmark was out of reach to begin with. It's a pity, really, to get to the end of a day and then focus only on what was left undone. There is more texture and variance to find and appreciate in any day than a checked-off to-do list can offer. There are myriad things that might have happened despite what we did or didn't do. There is far more life and vibrancy to discover in days that ebb and flow than in streamlined, optimised days. We forget we want the symphonies produced by the orchestra, not one flat note.

Just as recognising that happiness is one of many emotional states that ebb and flow, we can recognise that our days and how productive we are within them vary. We have bursts of productivity just as we have bursts of happiness. The ideal days where everything seems to fall into place are something we fall into, just like moments of happiness.

What if, instead of trying to optimise our days to do more, we allowed the days to unfold just as they are? We crowd our days with doing, ignoring how many extraneous components can take up the day too—going for a 30-minute run is rarely a neat 30 minutes: it can take hours by the time we finally ready ourselves to head out the door or attend to some more pressing task first, not to mention shower and get ready afterwards. Maybe the perfectly optimised among us don't dilly-dally or become distracted, but I'm yet to encounter such a person. If I did, I suspect they'd have sufficient resources—meaning money, support or perhaps a treadmill in their at-home gym—that their errands, the dashing back and forth, and the bits and pieces added to the day don't get in the way. But for the most part, being a fallible human means we need to recognise our own tendency to dawdle, to dash, to buffer the doing, whether out of necessity or habit—and maybe we don't need to add a layer of guilt, anxiety or shame to that. Perhaps, instead of trying to optimise, we can learn to reroute the guilt, anxiety and shame we encounter on *days like these* and accept ourselves as imperfect people simply experiencing the day.

Whether it's happiness, productivity or the ideal day, when we chase, grasp and expect, we inevitably fall short. We won't find the thing, the hack, the productivity tip that will magically make us feel whole and complete—because becoming whole and complete is an illusion. Instead, when we create space for our own imperfection, for the messiness in our days, we might just get the best out of them.

There's no doubt that on the days we do the thing, we feel good. There's a shimmer to those days when we've done something we've been putting off, and we wonder why we didn't do it earlier. Committing ourselves to do the thing can be the biggest hurdle, and the smug feeling that follows making a start or sustaining our effort is well earned. Doing can imbue the day with meaning. It can provide a focus, a challenge and a reprieve. It provides a forward motion to the day, to our lives. If we don't do anything, we don't enact change for ourselves and the world around us. Doing is walking the talk, it is action, it is putting ourselves into the world. So we don't want to forgo the doing, or give up the joy we feel on the days we did do the thing, but rather see that what we do in each day will look different.

We've mistaken doing things—being 'productive'—as the measure of a day well spent, when really that's just one of many by-products of living well. It's the way we define our lives by doing that needs a reshuffle: how we use doing to determine our worth, doing as a signpost for how much we matter, doing as a substitute for character—or not-doing as a mark of shame.

Being productive is difficult to define, after all. Is it about how long you work? Is it the quality of the work? Is it keeping busy at prescribed times? Is it efficiency? Is it significance? Is it the outcome? Is a productive day one when you hustled relentlessly, or is it one when you did something menial yet important? Productive work is not merely what makes us money, either. It also refers to the things that bring us emotional satisfaction or a sense of achievement—renovating a home, cooking for people we love, studying. Being unproductive is equally amorphous, especially as it can be the moments of idleness or rest that can yield insight, meaning and satisfaction, too.

If the root meaning of the word *productivity* is to 'lead something forward', then by this definition we are placed in a state of perpetual lurching—a checked-off to-do list that will fill up again the next day. Rather than trying to 'catch up' to something that is ceaselessly moving ahead of us, we must define our own version of 'enough'. We can find ways to untether from valuing our lives by how efficient, effective or ordered they are.

Perhaps we don't want to be more productive in our days, but more *fecund*—that is, more capable of producing new growth, but not always in producing mode. Seen in this light, our days are like fertile gardens: a place to plant, to sow, to weed, to prune, to pick, to compost, depending on the season. A fecund day will look different at different times: some days we did the thing, some days we didn't. There will be some fruits ripening, but there will also be weeds—distractions, unexpected calls, delays.

To be fecund, we need to be nourished. This view shifts the emphasis away from the things we accomplish and towards the things that feed us: how well we have slept, how dedicated we are to something, how kind, how assertive, how generous, how well we treat the people we love, how much we learn, how resilient we are. We so often overlook these parts of the day, but it's the very mulch that we need to yield growth.

Our days don't need to be optimised, but simply occupied—that is, lived in, tended to, renewed. The scramble of everyday life can render every discretionary hour as one to seize, but there will inevitably be moments we fail to grasp. My hunch is that we all have moments we faff and flounder—it's just so rare for people to admit that they do too.

But even in the uneventful days, where instead of doing the thing we set out to, we pottered or tooled around, we can find something nestled in the hours that's worthwhile. Maybe it didn't make us money or progress our career, but it too can imbue the day with meaning—a thought, a conversation with a friend as you're flopping on the couch, a new recipe to try, a walk outside, a smile from a stranger, taking a nap. Sometimes even a hangover can be a sign of a fun night with friends. Why can't these small things, too, be counted among the doing in our days?

Even though individual circumstances can be different, removing the judgement when a day—or even an hour—goes off track is something we can each practise. We can try to see that so often it's the unexpected, the unproductive, the imperfect that refreshes our days. Some days it's the thing we didn't think we'd have time for that turns out to be the very thing we needed. Some days might go by when we didn't do *the* thing, but we did that *other* thing that turns out to be just as important. Some days we do things and we're not quite sure why, only for it to all make sense at some future time.

Of course, on some days doing the thing is non-negotiable. It feels like a struggle just to keep up—either making us feel stifled by overwhelm or on the road to burnout. But whether we resent all that we have to do or lament what we haven't done, perhaps there's room for each of us to reshape how we measure the day. We need to dig up the stifling standards and instead plant something that is far more fitting in a world that requires empathy, flexibility and action. We need to find small, defiant acts against the idea that productivity is the sole measure of our worth. We need to inspire a gentler, more accepting approach to the ebb and flow of our days. We need to find our own way.

How we spend our days is how we ~~spend our lives~~ slowly figure out how to navigate our lives

From the outside looking in, it can appear as if everyone has it figured out, everyone is doing more, doing better and coping just fine. So why can't we do the thing?

Mystified by how other people seemed to effortlessly go about their days, in 2014 I set about asking people I admired what they did, how they did it and when they did it. I published the results on my labour of love, a blog called *Extraordinary Routines*, and later on my podcast, *Routines & Ruts*. The interview project was an attempt to find the remarkable in the everyday, a collection of hints to enable my own pursuit to do exceptional things amid the chaos of daily life. Speaking to those who seemed to have things figured out offered me a chance, I thought, to peek behind the highlight reel and receive guidance on how I too could become more productive, more successful, more prolific—how I could do more and be more. Such conversations even led me to devise experiments for myself—from testing out morning routines to switching off my devices.

But despite all my probing, I didn't arrive at a perfect recipe for getting things done. After more than half a decade of interviews and experiments, I still didn't feel like I was doing enough, doing it right, doing it well. With hindsight, I can see I kept falling into 'if only' spirals, because I was looking in the wrong direction for the answer. By requesting someone else's how-to manual, I was overlooking the need for me to navigate my own life.

It's not an exercise I lament, however. It took asking people about the everyday reality of their lives for me to realise we can't expect to re-create the same recipe when we don't have same ingredients. We each have our own capabilities, energy, aptitudes, privileges and available hours in the day, and these just don't look the same for everyone. The ability to optimise your day varies greatly if you're a freelancer, unemployed, a gig worker, executive assistant, student or working parent. The minutiae of our daily lives differ for each of us, yet we often compare ourselves with others—and wind up feeling worse.

It would be remiss of me not to acknowledge how much my investigating of people's daily routines may perpetuate this very pedestalling of getting things done. A written profile and a podcast conversation can only reveal so much, and certainly not all the foibles of a life. But for me these conversations reaffirmed that there is a plethora of ways we can go about our days—and the most important way is one that is our own and that we can adjust accordingly.

While I started out asking how people do what they do, what became more interesting to me was hearing about the stumbles. If there was a resounding insight I gained after sifting through people's days, it's that nobody has all the answers, nobody knows what they're doing, and everybody is looking at everybody else, trying to keep up, adjusting where necessary. We all stumble, we all make mistakes, we all have days where we didn't do the thing.

For me, these imperfect fragments of people's days began to form a mosaic—a reminder that the mess and muck look different for everyone. This book is a celebration of those fragments, of the days we stumble but find something to appreciate all the same. It's a collection of my own notes from those conversations, the moments of insight, and words from books, commencement speeches, films and people that have helped me navigate the obstacles of productivity guilt, and what's helped me let go. It's written as I keep stumbling, keep learning, keep guessing and keep asking questions, and even keep changing my answers. I'm fumbling through too, and I want to share what I've learned along the way.

That's another important note: as an interviewer, I bring myself and my own lens to each conversation. This is obvious from the people I interviewed, the questions I asked, the topics I was drawn to. The project itself is not an exhaustive survey of daily life—it was a passion project I did on the side of paid employment when I could, where I could, with people I could have the chance to speak to. It was approached in fits and starts when I had the time, space and inclination. Throughout the endeavour, I have brought my own limited view and privileged circumstances—the privilege of education, of being able to determine my own career, of saving for travel, of choosing to work less and live frugally so I can follow my creative endeavours, of benefiting from the very capitalist structures I stumble over.

The answers I collected reflect where I was at with my own relationship to doing. I was fascinated in particular by creative people, those whom I saw constructing the day for themselves either as freelancers, artists or entrepreneurs. I asked questions where I was hoping to see myself reflected in the answers. At different times I was navigating a full-time job, freelance work or part-time work, trying to figure out a way to swing into my own days that wasn't tethered to productivity or output, and sometimes swinging right back, depending on my circumstances.

Instead of gleaning directions for doing things, over time I began to see shared feelings in my interviewees—many felt they weren't doing enough, or felt uncertain, unsure if they'd ever get there. Seeing these feelings in others has helped me feel less alone as I navigate this doing-obsessed world, and I hope you too might find similar comfort among the pages of this book.

In this way, this book is not science-backed, but rather feeling-backed. The ideas, circumstances or insights I share may not be a one-to-one translation of your experience, but I know I've found lessons from people different from me to be nevertheless meaningful. There can be solace in finding something to share with others, and in broadening our perspective. We can be interested in what it's like to be someone else, and often find parts of ourselves in them, too. Each chapter explores a stumbling block of productivity that we can tumble over in our days. This is not to denounce these aspects of our lives, but rather to unravel the feelings of self-blame we can have when we encounter them. As standalone components of a day, we may not find something like ambition or balance to be negative, but when we pursue them rigidly we can find ourselves hurled into the 'if only' spiral. We may also find that these stumbles can have a knock-on effect: our ambitions for the future can make us busier in the present, so we long for a sense of balance that's unattainable or fleeting, or we add expectations to the day that will only leave us disappointed.

Rather than offering up an answer or formula to smooth over the missteps in your days, I hope this book might serve as a companion as you experience the 'if only' spiral, and guide you to your own thinking, your own feeling, your own way. Each of the following chapters can be a place you dip in and dip out of, depending on your daily tumbles. Perhaps it might serve as a reminder that a tumble doesn't have to be painful—it can be playful. We can learn, we can inspect what we're feeling, and we might even find ourselves enjoying the somersault.

Reader, I cannot promise that you will do more in your day after reading this book, but I hope it might encourage you to embrace your own way of doing things, rather than follow another prescription that only sets you up to fail. I hope it means you continue to relish the days you did the thing, but also to find something to celebrate on the days you didn't—because we will continue to experience both as our lives ebb and flow.

While we can look to others for inspiration, we are the only ones who live our days. How we navigate our days is how we learn to navigate our lives. It takes us a long time to figure out how to realise our wants, to find our own recipe for a day, and to be okay when that looks different to somebody else's. Sometimes, without the bumpers of someone else's instructions, we can feel we are cutting corners, stumbling without directions or going off track, but that's where we can find our own way. That's how we get to know all sides of the fallible, messy, imperfect human that we are—instead of waiting to be told what to do, we make it up as we go along and keep reshaping the parts of our day.

If the conversations I've had have taught me one thing, it's that our cracks are what make us far more relatable and interesting and form the most beautiful mosaic. The part that doesn't always get things done. The part that wants to change. The part that's trying to untangle itself from always needing to change something. The part that is still figuring things out. They're the parts that remind us there is so much more to the day than doing.

2

The Expansion of Creativity

*So, from my point of view . . . I see your life as already artful,
waiting, just waiting and ready for you to make it art.*

Toni Morrison, commencement address to the
Wellesley College class of 2004

If our days have become crowded containers for what we did or
did not do, perhaps we do not need to pursue more ways to be
productive, but rather shake up the contents.

I've had too many days to count that have been flattened by
productivity guilt. They follow a pattern: there is *the thing* I should
be doing, but for whatever reason I find myself not doing *the thing*
at *this time*, so instead I don't do *anything*. Instead of turning my
attention to something else that can be done, the day seems to
evaporate as I sit, stifled by the taunt, *I didn't do the thing today,
I didn't do the thing today*. Wouldn't it be more satisfying to at least
try to enjoy the day instead of washing it away with guilt?

Productivity is too narrow a lens for our days. It flattens the day to a plan, an order, an outcome. When the day takes a different shape, we find ourselves coiled in a spiral, narrowing in on ourselves and our shortcomings.

Productivity tells us to live sequentially, but our days rarely unfold in perfect order. Not only does each day vary, but we vary within them. We are constantly shifting, creating and re-creating parts of ourselves. I have come to see the value in being more flexible with the order and shape of things: I can see what I have done, or what I can do differently, or what can still be done later. I can find ways to expand my day beyond a *certain kind of doing* and define my own process.

If productivity narrows our days, creativity expands them. Creativity doesn't follow a plan, but has its own ebb and flow. Instead of confining a day to doing, it enlivens us to the ways we can *do it differently*.

Creativity can be the antidote to the anxiety, guilt and shame we can encounter because it responds to what arises in our day rather than prescribes it. The creative process itself reflects this. In his book *The Art of Thought*, British psychologist Graham Wallas outlined the four stages of the creative process. There's the preparation stage, where we gather inspiration and research; the incubation stage, where we step away and allow connections to simmer; the illumination stage, where a solution often spontaneously arrives in an 'aha' moment; and the verification stage, where we take necessary action and do the thing.

There's no checklist for the creative process, but rather a constant oscillation among these various stages—and arguably many others. In this non-linear cycle of gathering, stepping away, arriving and doing, we can take away our self-judgement about where we are at and allow for a natural ebb and flow. Instead of rushing to the part when we are 'done' or discarding fragments of our day just because there isn't a clear link to output, creativity can help us embrace what is not yet done. In place of the guilt, anxiety or shame we might feel when we didn't do the thing, we have a more malleable, flexible and open guide for our days.

With the creative process in mind, we can listen to the call of what needs to be done during the different phases, irrespective of whether the thing we need to do is considered creative or not. This allows us to cultivate curiosity as we gather, to be comfortable with uncertainty as we step away, to be patient as we await a solution, and to show up when there is something that must be done.

Even if we're not doing the thing we're meant to be doing, this doesn't mean we're not doing the important work of preparing to do the thing. In this we can see the importance of getting away from the desk and into the world. Where a productivity lens may mean that waiting in line at a supermarket looks like time spent inefficiently, a creativity lens can reveal the importance of cultivating patience, tolerance and curiosity in all the in-between moments of our days.

Often a solution can't be rushed or planned for; instead, the best ideas and connections may catch us by surprise. When we are stuck on a thing, instead of spiralling we can give ourselves permission to turn to something else instead.

We can see that doing the thing is just one part of the process— and it often follows its own timeline. There will be times when we want to rush to do the thing as if it's a new romance, and times when we are going to fall out of love and perhaps even hate the thing. There is always a part in the creative process when we wish to give up entirely—but that part is integral if we want to create something worthwhile. It's only by tumbling through this love and this hate of a thing that we can engage with all its parts and transform it into something new.

Living creatively, then, means to live flexibly and openly, not sequentially. It means embracing creative tension because it's the very thing that makes the orchestra so captivating—varying notes, voices, sounds. It means being creative with all that we encounter, including our stumbles.

We can each be day artists

You don't need to be 'a creative' to live a creative life. Applying the creative process as a lens to our lives simply means a day doesn't have to be narrowed by productivity, but rather observed and shaped depending on what's in front of us—much like a potter at a wheel.

Being creative, I think, has less to do with your job title or some artistic pursuit, and everything to do with how you shape your own life—how you turn your attention to another thing, instead of lamenting the thing you didn't do. Spending the better part of a decade interviewing artists, designers, musicians and thinkers about their creative processes hasn't rendered me artistically prolific by any stretch—I can't recall the last time I picked up a paintbrush— but just because I'm not a painter, that doesn't mean I can't live like one. Creativity isn't reserved to a select few—we all have access to this innately human trait. It's a great loss to us all, in fact, to confine it to a particular subset of people who have had access to certain education or the means—in time, money or luck—to follow their passions and purpose. We might not even know what our passions and purpose are, but we can still see creativity as a human aspiration accessible to us all.

Creativity is present in the ways we get to know ourselves, express ourselves, question what we believe in, discover what we want—it's in how we live our lives. As the novelist Henry Miller put it, 'To make living itself an art, that is the goal.'

We live our lives as if they are a script, but we can improvise—we can go with the moment, we can find something new, we can be curious about what's right in front of us. We seem to forget that we can be creative with at least part of our schedules, our careers, our conversations, our definitions of balance, ambition and enjoyment.

We don't have to make grand creative gestures to find poetry in our daily lives—we can simply try something new or see something anew. It can be appreciating something in the day that already exists, or reshaping it to suit us. To borrow a quote attributed to the actress Helena Bonham Carter, everything in life is art: 'What you do. How you dress. The way you love someone, and how you talk. Your smile and your personality. What you believe in, and all your dreams. The way you drink your tea. How you decorate your home. Or party. Your grocery list. The food you make. How your writing looks. And the way you feel. Life is art.'

Each of us creates our day through how we interact with the world, with ourselves, with other people. If we see creativity as a way of *being* rather than of *doing*, we can attempt to live each day as if our life itself is a work of art—we can be what I like to call 'day artists'. To me, being a day artist affirms that creativity isn't just something we do—it's how we live our lives. When I first put the words 'day' and 'artist' together, it made me chuckle because it reminded me of a worker at a fast-food chain who might call themselves a 'sandwich artist'. Some would say both pairings are grandiose—almost anyone can make a sandwich, everyone has a day, so who are you to deem yourself an artist when your material is so commonplace? But that's precisely the point. If we don't play with what we have at our disposal, how can we find enjoyment in the mundanity of our daily lives? We're so used to the wonder that is a day that we call it ordinary. Perhaps reminding ourselves what an extraordinary thing it is to have a day—a day where anything can happen—is a better goal than trying to optimise and render it perfect. As G.K. Chesterton said in *Tremendous Trifles*, 'The world will never starve for want of wonders; but only for want of wonder.'

A day artist is the light-hearted counterpart to the strict optimiser of days. We should look to artists not merely for advice on how to create something astounding, but also for the insights they have when it comes to dismantling the constraints of a productivity-obsessed culture: how to go with the ebb and flow of the creative process, how to work within constraints, how to find what works for us day by day, hour by hour, even minute by minute.

Our approach to work, life, relationships and even our own definitions of productivity can benefit from the application of these creative lessons. Even those whose days are more regimented than those of the self-directed artist can learn from the insights. We too can reject the status quo, act on our wants, say yes more, learn when to say no, take things step by step, allow for space, embrace mistakes and be open to the inevitable ups and downs of life, the successes and failures, the potential of both the done and the not-yet-done.

We can see what we need to thrive rather than change. Through the lens of a day artist, we can see what's needed in our own process— it may be a deadline, or moments of downtime, or not setting a morning alarm, or setting a dozen in five-minute increments.

A day artist isn't defined by their work, but rather immersed in it. Rather than having a set routine from which they will inevitably slip, the day artist finds rhythms. The day artist is more than the doing—they are the choreographer of their ideas, the composer of their inner life and the curator of their experiences. Being a day artist takes the judgement away from the different versions of our days: there's something to glean equally from the dull days, the joyous days, the unproductive days, the changing days—because each day can be an experiment.

Experimenting with our day is an act of applying our human creativity. It's less about doing more than about doing things more creatively—which means embracing messiness and imperfection. The people I've interviewed have taught me to find joy in the process rather than the outcome. They lean into the dread of doing the thing to find flow. They create beauty from entangled human emotions. The rut becomes a lesson. Comparison becomes a guide. *Shoulds* are replaced with *wants*. Distraction is a place for discovery.

When we strip back judgement of what we did or didn't do, we can embrace the day for what it is—an empty canvas. We might not have the same privileges, the same resources, the same available hours in the day as somebody else, and our canvas will not look the same as theirs. But irrespective of our life circumstances, each of us is given a day, and within it there is always something, however small, we can experiment with.

We can strive to encounter everything a day offers—people, places, things, feelings, missteps—and reframe them for ourselves. It's this commitment to experimenting—to trying, to starting over—that can imbue our days with meaning, perhaps more than doing. As Ralph Waldo Emerson wrote in his journal, 'All life is an experiment. The more experiments you make the better.'

As day artists, we can treat life as one big experiment—to find what brings us alive, and have the courage to get closer to it so it can expand us. We can try new things, follow whims, focus on discovery, build patience, allow surprises to happen. We can trust, hold things lightly, take the pressure off. We can be okay with the not-quite-theres, with the change-of-minds. When we treat our days like an experiment, we see it's all part of the process—the failures, mistakes and stumbles come with the territory. And those stumbles can help us deal with the knocks of daily life. As Emerson added, 'What if you do fail, and get fairly rolled in the dirt once or twice? Up again, you shall never be so afraid of a tumble.' Each tumble in our days is an opportunity to learn, so we do not fall so hard the next time.

It will not be the same each day—neither what brings us alive, nor what knocks us about. But making creativity rather than productivity the focus of our day helps us become more open to accepting this version of the day and what we do within it. We can let more of life unfold and learn from the tangles. We can experiment with the best way to live, dabbing a little bit of under-standing here, a little bit of softness there—to paint a more vibrant picture for ourselves, and for people around us. We can remind ourselves that we do not find the way; we create it continuously.

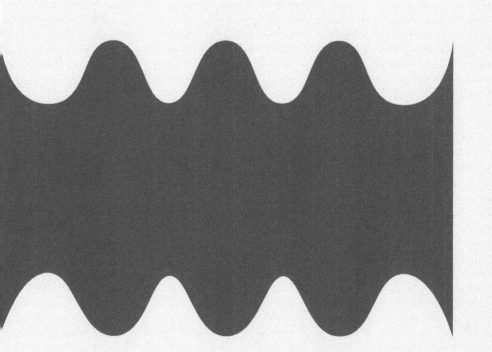

The Stumbles in the Day

3

The Hopeless Search for the Ideal Routine

A schedule defends from chaos and whim. It is a net for catching days. It is a scaffolding on which a worker can stand and labour with both hands at sections of time.

Annie Dillard, *The Writing Life*

Sometimes we need the support of a schedule to catch our days. Routines appear solid. They promise order. They seem reliable. They can be comforting. A routine can provide a sense of certainty and control in a world that is uncertain and outside our control. But there are days we can just as easily become entangled in the net of a schedule, or find ourselves slipping through its holes.

The pressure to optimise our days has led some of us to revere elaborate routines to the point they've become precarious structures built atop our aspirations to be better. Personally, I've long made a pastime of drafting ideal daily routines for myself, filling row after row of my notepad with perfectly timed steps, convinced that if I could just get my routine right, I could get my life right.

Tomorrow—according to one draft—I will get up at sunrise and journal for 30 minutes, before doing a series of dynamic stretches while I listen to an inspiring podcast, and then set out for a leisurely jog. Returning home, I'll mindfully brew a coffee and have a healthy breakfast while I read a poem. By 8.30 am, I will be sitting down at my desk to commence a four-hour deep-work session, with well-timed breaks throughout where I will do push-ups, star-jumps or eye stretches. I will stay hydrated. I'll sip herbal tea. At lunch, I'll eat a bowl of brown rice and nourishing greens, before going for a brisk walk, call a friend, read the news and check social media in the ten minutes I've allotted, no more. I'll be back at my desk by one o'clock and attend to administration, emails, pressing calls, lingering to-dos. The evening I'll spend with friends, laughing around a dinner table, or on a date that's going swimmingly, or maybe I'll see a film or a talk by someone prominent and wise, or attend a networking event and charm strangers. I won't drink too much wine or stay out too late. If I'm staying in for some designated solitude, I'll work on a side project, learn a new skill, immerse myself in something meaningful. I won't shilly-shally the evening hours away trying to pick a new series to binge. By nine in the evening, I will switch off all electronic devices. I will bathe and apply various serums and creams in the correct order. I will write three things I'm grateful for. Then I will get into bed with a book, no phone within reach. I will set my analogue alarm clock for six o'clock. I will repeat this the next day, and for the rest of my perfectly optimised life.

When the actual tomorrow arrives and I've missed a single step in this carefully constructed sequence—say, I've snoozed through an ambitiously early alarm—the entire structure topples over like a tower of Jenga blocks. Instead of making the adjustments necessary to carry on with the day, I'll chide myself for the mess I've made. I couldn't possibly do my morning pages in the midmorning, so I skip them entirely, along with my morning jog. Already I'm feeling behind on all that I set for myself, and the day disappears in a haze of distraction, scrambling or faffing. Nothing feels 'just right'—so, I tell myself, I may as well wait for tomorrow and start all over again.

For some of us, when things fall through the net and we don't stick to our ideal routine—because of bosses, because of kids, because of a sunny afternoon, because of life—we enter the 'if only' spiral. Instead of inspecting the precarious structure we've tried to assemble, we might draft another new routine—perhaps one that is even more elaborate or strict—and convince ourselves that it's topple-proof.

What we are really doing is setting ourselves up to fail. With a rigid idea of how things should be, we can easily find an excuse to strike out an entire day. We let the slight detour at the beginning prevent us from resuming the course.

My penchant for trying to perfect my routine—and the resulting shame I felt for perpetually failing—led me to interview hundreds of people about how they construct their days. I was on the outside looking in at their seemingly perfectly placed Jenga towers, searching for secrets I could use as my own. But when I stepped inside and inspected their days, I soon found that no one's wooden blocks are as perfectly stacked as they may appear.

It turns out I was not alone in dropping the pieces in an effort to get my day to stack up. Even if someone is in tune with how they work best, rarely does anyone perfectly adhere to a perfect routine. What I observed among many I interviewed were the same two versions of a day I was grappling with: the ideal routine we draft for ourselves, where productivity is optimised, distractions are minimised and our output is at a maximum—and then the messy, everyday reality of our days as they unfold. Rarely is the aspirational ideal achieved; on most days we are adjusting, tumbling and rebuilding.

In our culture that is obsessed with productivity, we tend to glorify routines and those who claim they can adhere to them perfectly. A routine is often touted as the salve to all kinds of dilemmas. Lost your job? Stick to your routine. Experiencing anxiety, depression or grief? Find a routine. Living through a pandemic? Get a new routine. But a routine is rarely the grand solution it promises to be, because it's so hard to always uphold one in particular.

Part of our routine problem is that we have taken things too far. When there's a structure to a day, it's true that many of us will feel more at ease, less overwhelmed by choice—we can ritualise the ordinary parts of life to make room for the extraordinary. We have a bedrock for the day so we can do things in ways and at times that prevent us from needing to think about or even remember doing them. That's why Barack Obama only wore blue and grey suits during his presidency: he didn't want to waste time or energy making a decision. But when we create a complicated ideal regime that accounts for every parcel of the day in the hope of getting more done, we exhaust ourselves. The idealised routine that many of us hold in our minds—or in the pages of our notebooks—is what leads us astray. We tell ourselves that to get the most out of our days, we must wake up early, diligently complete our tasks, squeeze the most from each hour. Despite the potential such an optimised routine has to make us prolific and productive, it's a false promise, because it's so rare we stick to it.

And perhaps we shouldn't be expected to. There are many reasons we may not be able to uphold a glorified or elaborate routine. Not everyone can exercise in their lunchbreak, sleep eight hours a night or afford a nanny. Our ability to control our day also varies greatly if we're a freelancer, gig worker, executive assistant or working parent. Time is a luxury that many people don't have—and so is a routine.

Maybe a routine is not always the perfect vessel for holding the day's variances, and our own. After finding out that so few people's days follow a set routine, my suspicion is that people are simply touting the importance of routine without upholding one in their own lives. I'm fond of a quote from poet Thom Gunn from a 1995 interview with *The Paris Review*: 'When anybody says, do you have a routine, I always say piously it's very important to have one, but in fact I don't.'

The aspirational routine to which we're pinning our hopes of being better is more like a mirage. Although we strive for it, we rarely reach what it promises, and the reason for this is the variance inherent in our days—in our energy, in our interests, in our interactions, in our everyday chaos. A perfectly ordered life will always remain outside the imperfect reality of our daily lives.

We can place so much emphasis on adhering to an aspirational order of things, but often the day has other ideas. We shouldn't bear yet another layer of guilt, anxiety or shame because we haven't followed a routine that might have been too stringent in the first place.

Coming to terms with the days that go off track does not mean resigning ourselves to a life of aimlessness, but rather acknowledging that having our Jenga towers topple over isn't a moral failing—it's simply part of the game. If we don't let a pile of wooden blocks on the floor spoil the games night with friends, why are we letting our inevitable tumbles ruin our days? Imagine if we overlooked the joy of the moment, of playing, laughing, concentrating, working together, because something that's designed to topple over did, in fact, topple over?

Do we really want a totally streamlined day, or do we want the variance that comes with being in tune with the ebb and flow of life? When you think about it, a perfectly ordered life—the one all the life hacks and listicles promise—would be a rather dull one. Routine is monotonous. Scheduling every moment of our day leaves no space for delight, joy, rapture, emotion, loafing, possibility. Optimised lives are unrelatable—if my elaborate draft proves anything.

The best days, I find, aren't the ones where I've crossed everything off a to-do list or adhered to the perfect schedule, but where I've experienced a surprise, a flirtation, a new idea, an encounter with flow. Only when the tower has fallen over can we appreciate each individual piece, instead of focusing only on how perfectly they might stack up.

When a routine meets a rut

Creating the ideal routine can, rather ironically, be the very thing that lands us in a rut. A thing that was providing momentum starts to feel tired, the pursuit of improving ourselves makes us feel exhausted, the chasing of better becomes boring.

A rut is a pattern of behaviour that has become dull and unproductive—and with that definition, can't we say the very same thing about a routine, which is, after all, merely a sequence of actions regularly followed?

When we find a rhythm that works for us, we have momentum. But over time that very rhythm settles into monotony: the path becomes so worn that we can find ourselves stuck in a rut. We might strive for the optimised day, but when we reach it— if we ever do, that is—it will eventually make us feel stagnant. A steady routine can begin to feel like an unrelenting Groundhog Day. While we glorify routines, we tend to judge being in a rut. But just as a schedule can provide comfort, a rut can alert us to when comfort has become inertia. Disruption brings new possibilities—in how we interact with our day, a particular situation or the people around us. As Leo Tolstoy put it in *War and Peace*, 'Once we're thrown off our habitual paths, we think all is lost; but it's only here that the new and the good begins. As long as there's life, there's happiness. There's much, much still to come.'

We need to find ourselves in the rut in order to notice that things are not as we want them to be—our work, our relationship, our living situation, our approach to our days—and something new and good can begin.

If we didn't have the rut, we would remain on autopilot, unchanging, unalert to new possibilities. For this reason, a rut isn't something we need to shy away from or rid from our lives—but rather something that can reveal to us a new way forward, and even prompt us to introduce variety back into our days.

We can rarely force ourselves out of a rut; we'd simply become further wedged. Instead, we need to be patient and curious, and reflect on where we are in order to find a new way forward. We might have a period of shutting down and doing very little— we might retreat from socialising or activities we'd usually enjoy, for instance. Simple tasks suddenly require more energy and effort, so we minimise what we do to sustain our energy.

We no doubt feel stuck when we're in a rut, but we can slowly retool ourselves towards a new way and adapt. I remember listening to the podcast *This Jungian Life*, where this process of adaptation was compared to making butter from heavy cream—you shake and you shake and you shake and nothing happens, so you shake and shake and shake some more, and suddenly you have butter. Moving out from a rut is similar: we have to work at it for a long time, sometimes repeating the same action or feeling like nothing is making a difference, feeling like we're stuck in the churn of it all, and finally we arrive at something new. Such a transition can be tiresome or discombobulating, but it's how our days are eventually refreshed with change.

Sometimes being in a rut can be the making of us. As I learned from the writings of Joseph Campbell, where you stumble, there lies your treasure. Ruts are often a prequel to change—something nudges us when we are in the rut and we find our way out. Sometimes

I DIDN'T DO THE THING TODAY

the sudden realisation one unfulfilling Tuesday afternoon that we're in a rut can be enough of a nudge. Other times, the nudge comes from outside us—it might be a bereavement, a breakup, an illness, a job loss, a disappointment, a rejection. A life milestone can be a nudge, or an interruption to our usual way of doing things—falling in love, the birth of a child, a new job, finishing school.

All these nudges can prompt us to ask who we are and what we want out of life. As the social researcher and author of *The Kindness Revolution* Hugh Mackay told me, 'The more we learn about human psychology, the more we realise that change, uncertainty, unpredictability, disruptions, unexpected events crashing into our lives help us to clarify this deeper sense of who we are and what we need to contribute to life.'

This isn't to glorify the pain and suffering we can experience from the different kinds of ruts we encounter in our days—rarely do we enjoy such experiences at the time—but we can perhaps pin some hope to the fact that on the other side there is often something new awaiting. At the very least, we can be sure to meet a new version of ourselves: one with more experience, one with a changed perspective, one who has been able to restore through being still or enduring the churn.

While a rut can be a great catalyst for change in our days, sometimes the nudge doesn't arrive and we remain stuck. We may want to remain wedged, sink deeper, spiral. We might start out doing fewer things so we can rest, but over time find it harder to do anything at all. Withdrawing from the world can make it difficult to return to it.

If we don't experience a nudge, perhaps we can engineer it. We can all get habituated, which means it's easier to overlook what's constant and pay more attention to what's novel—whether that's something good or bad. So, by that logic, moving patiently out of the rut requires we do something different—we must move when we have stagnated.

Yet moving may be the last thing we feel like doing. For the times we cannot summon the motivation to move, we can perhaps just shift ever so slightly. As Washington Irving wrote in *Tales of a Traveller*, 'There is a certain relief in change, even though it be from bad to worse; as I have found in travelling in a stage-coach, that it is often a comfort to shift one's position and be bruised in a new place.' A slight shift or nudge can be uncomfortable because we don't always know we are experiencing change—we keep adjusting and bruising in new places, unsure why whatever we do keeps hurting. We can't always see that we are in the valley— it simply feels like the world is moving on without us. But it's the willingness to shift even when it's uncomfortable that can help us see that we will once again reach the peak. From my own experience, and from my conversations with others, it is when we remain open to shifting and adjusting that we eventually find ourselves in a new position where we find a rhythm once more. As the author and artist Mari Andrew told me after experiencing a string of heartbreak and grief, 'I wanted to find ways to make myself happy and mentally strong. All of that was done through routine—drawing once a day, taking guitar lessons twice a week, doing yoga, waking up earlier, even just learning how to do my hair in new ways.'

That's what I find fascinating—a routine can be the thing that gets us into a rut, but it can also be what brings us out of one. Such shifts happen on a granular level—in the sleep we get, exercise, eating well, a creative outlet—and can be the very things that form a new routine. Instead of getting entangled or tumbling over the ideal version of a routine, we can see individual components as supports, and nudge ourselves on until they feel more comfortable. Over time, we might start to recognise what we can rely on—time spent with certain people, enough sleep, enjoyable activities, places, rituals, even books can all become like pillars for the difficult days. It can take us a long time to learn what we need to keep momentum, or what steadies us—and it often changes. Maybe we need to underscore the importance of scattering different building blocks across different parts of our lives. Rather than funnelling our entire sense of self into one thing, one focus, one goal, we can scatter it across our lives so that the tumbles don't throw us off course completely. After a bad day at work, a ceramics class or a visit to the local pool or a drink with a friend might be what helps you remain upright.

As the writer and broadcaster Benjamin Law told me, 'Often when we've invested so much of our sense of wellbeing, so much of our sense of worth, into these singular goals, we forget that there are other, smaller things that are just as important—spending time with your family, exercising, trying out the new recipe that you've wanted to try for a really long time.'

This, to me, is what self-care looks like. Because caring is not about fixing completely; rather, it's a work in progress of fostering, trusting and shifting position as necessary. To care doesn't have to be costly and prescriptive—it's often the mundane things that provide a sense of agency to move towards a new rhythm in our days. So a slight shift when we're in a rut can be as simple as going back to basics. Tidying your sock drawer might give you a sense of control. It might be exercising when you'd prefer not to. It might be seeing a friend, or protecting your solitude. It might be doing hard things, like making apologies and forgiving yourself, or arranging your finances. It might be getting enough sleep. It might be putting clean sheets on your bed. It might be taking a nap and not feeling guilty about it. Self-care is often also a private moment—not a bubble bath that we want to share on social media, but an ordinary act that brings us back to ourselves or introduces us to a new version of ourselves.

We rarely find ourselves immediately springing into action after a rut. We are often nudged through intermediate stages of two steps forward, one step back—but we eventually find our way. In this continuous cycle of the routine, the rut, the nudge, we eventually find ourselves once again with a new rhythm to our days—we settle into a new home, we ease into a new job, we start dating again, we feel a sense of possibility for a different future, we feel the strength of our perseverance.

Naturally, our entire lives don't turn over in a perfect sequence— while we may have a new-found sense of momentum in our work, we might be stuck in a rut in our relationship. At other times it can feel as if we meet rut after rut after rut. Our days are made up of peaks and troughs, stops and starts, and sometimes of long stretches of stagnation. We don't need to apply judgement to one phase or glorify another—we can simply allow ourselves to be in the part of the cycle we are always moving through. As the novelist Haruki Murakami wrote in *The Wind-Up Bird Chronicle*, 'The point is, not to resist the flow. You go up when you're supposed to go up and down when you're supposed to go down. When you're supposed to go up, find the highest tower and climb to the top. When you're supposed to go down, find the deepest well and go down to the bottom. When there's no flow, stay still.'

We will always find ourselves in the cycle, shifting through the stages—but knowing this can help you get through the current ebb, and trust that there will once again be flow. Often, when we create space in our days for listening to our needs, when we persevere with the churn, when we allow for the nudges, we find there is still so much life to live between the rut and the rhythm.

Maybe you're higgledy-piggledy, too

After many years of drafting new routines, interviewing hundreds of people about theirs, reading countless productivity books and conducting self-devised experiments, I still haven't acquired a routine.

When I faced the fact that I'm not a person with a set routine, I was able to see with clarity that it wasn't my inability to stick to a routine that was the problem, but rather my obsession with trying to achieve the ideal. In my hopeless search for the perfect routine, I found a new hope: that it's possible to enrich our days without the elaborate netting. I stopped collecting habits and hacks, and started to collect reminders from people I interviewed that helped me embrace my own shambolic schedule: someone would tell me, 'Every day is different.' Another would say, 'I'm a mixed bag,' or 'I struggle with having routine more than not having one.'

Routines are not for everyone. There's nothing inherently better about being someone who can stick to a routine. It doesn't make you smarter, more likeable, more fulfilled, more generous. Besides, as the musician Ella Hooper reminded me, a routine isn't always filled with 'good' habits: 'I do have some things that I do every day—and they are mainly my foibles.'

By that logic, there's nothing inferior about being someone who doesn't have a routine. In fact, as I've observed, we can fold our own version of joy, discipline and contentment into our days without one.

Speaking with fashion designer Jenny Kee crystalised for me that it's okay to be 'higgledy-piggledy'. Recovering from a back injury and adrenal fatigue, she told me she needs to spend the majority of her week without a routine in order to be open to the pendulum swing her health might create with her days: 'I'm higgledy-piggledy, but that's how I am. I like my day to be a bit free. I'm nearly 70 and I don't think it's going to change!'

Instead of berating ourselves for not sticking to a routine, what if we were simply okay with not having one? What if we did away with the elaborate schedules we draft for ourselves? What if we swapped hard rules for elastic possibilities? After all, as long as you're attending to the day you're in—and the sometimes moveable feast of work schedules, family-life commitments and personal pursuits—is the order in which the day unfolds really something to judge so harshly?

I'm slowly replacing my ideal routines with openness towards different versions of the day, and the possibilities that can come with starting it from scratch. We are always, after all, starting each day from scratch. Not in the sense that the day is void of commitments, but in that we do not know what will come of the day. We can sometimes have a routine, sometimes not. We can have some constants and some changes. We can have periods of flux. We can have moments where we wish we meditated more or exercised every day. We can try to build a net for catching our days, but also know that life will sometimes feel more like a trembling Jenga tower.

Realising that my natural tendency is to be a bit higgledy-piggledy has helped ease my feelings of anxiety, guilt and shame for not sticking to a routine. Interestingly, when I stopped trying to negate the variances of a day, I found myself more engaged, even more—perish the thought—productive. But perhaps that shouldn't be surprising—often when we accept ourselves, we are more likely to get the best from ourselves. Taking away the self-judgements allows us to look at what we need to thrive instead of what we need to change. Instead of trying to force myself into becoming a morning person with a dreadfully early alarm and then berating myself for pressing the snooze button, I can face the fact that I'm probably never going to be part of the 5 am club, and instead get the sleep my body needs. The net, I've learned, is something I found myself resistant to—when I tell myself I must do something, I find that I don't want to do it. This is often referred to as psychological reactance, or the negative knee-jerk reaction to being told what to do, even if we are the ones telling ourselves to do it.

Maybe you're similarly routine-resistant. Many of us may feel more like ourselves when we go with the drift of the day—even within a structure imposed on us, we might be the kind to search for some room to manoeuvre as our energy and attention waxes and wanes. What we *have to do* varies for each of us, depending on whether we have a nine-to-five job (or perhaps a second job), whether we have children, or a partner, or someone we care for. But even if different parts of our days must incorporate things we have to do, we might find the best way to approach the day is to wriggle within the bits we can.

After all, we don't just pull a routine onto our days like a jumper—it's a constant knitting and unstitching to find something that suits us. Every habit or routine fits people differently at different times, and we all have different strengths, desires, body clocks, energy levels, talents and interests. It's also a constant reshaping— we can keep the routines we need, shed the ones we don't, embed new ones when we do.

We reach for routine because we think it will help instil in us a sense of control, and maybe that's true for some people. But flexibility can accomplish the same for others. As the illustrator Marc Martin told me, 'Being flexible with times and routines helps me feel in control of my life.'

Speaking to the milliner Richard Nylon, I learned that it's possible to shrug it off when things don't fit in their allotted hour, rather than spiral for not doing the thing: 'I know there are people who really thrive off having this done at that hour, and they get annoyed if this or that isn't happening, or if something doesn't go to plan it tends to upset them,' he told me. 'Whereas if something doesn't happen, I just shrug my shoulders and get on with it.'

Instead of trying to play catch-up, maybe we should simply shrug and get on with it. Doing so can open us up to possibility. It shifts the focus from what we didn't do today to what can happen today. Our output ebbs and flows, too, depending on the task at hand: sometimes we seem to get so much out of a day; sometimes we don't know where the day went. As Thom Gunn went on to say after admitting to not having a routine, 'It's been my experience that sometimes about ten poems will all come in about two months; other times it will be that one poem will take ages and ages to write.' Creativity doesn't follow a perfectly consistent schedule, and being the creative bunch of day artists that we are, perhaps neither should we. As Maya Angelou said in *Wouldn't Take Nothing for My Journey Now*, 'Because of the routines we follow, we often forget that life is an ongoing adventure.' The sooner we realise or perhaps remember this, said Angelou, the sooner we will treat our life as art: 'To bring all our energies to each encounter, to remain flexible enough to notice and admit when what we expected to happen did not happen. We need to remember that we are created creative and can invent new scenarios as frequently as they are needed.'

Rather than be bowled over by our higgledy-piggledy rhythms, we can learn to go with them—to see them as an ongoing adventure, and even create new scenarios when we need them. We can learn to trust that the work will get done when the work gets done. We can be alive to the times we briskly do the things, and to the times things can be slower. We can turn our attention to what we want from the hour, rather than what the hour wants from us.

That said, even when we embrace that routine is not for us, we may still need structures to help us do the things we want to do in the hours. While having no set pattern can bring more freedom, it also brings uncertainty-fuelled anxiety. It can be a difficult task to create our patterns on our own—perhaps this is why it can be hard to meet our own deadlines. So how do we best set ourselves up to do the thing without creating the same rigid ideals we tumble over?

In place of elaborate routines, many people I've interviewed create anchors that can be flexible within the day. The most memorable may be the 'portable routine' of artist and author Austin Kleon. On any given day, he aims to journal, write, read and walk. Those activities don't follow a particular order, nor do they always happen, but when he does those four things, it's a good day.

This checklist approach can also help compound momentum. In Austin's example, he writes a short blog post each day, which goes into his weekly newsletter. Over time, he starts to notice themes forming, which may develop into a talk, and that talk might become the foundation for a book. One ticked checkbox fuels others, while offering small rewards along the way. So maybe that's where we start—not with a perfectly ordered routine, but with a checklist of small things that we can do each day to make it a good day.

Our days improve not because things are done in perfect order, but when we are present to whatever is in them. Sometimes that means leaving a checkbox unticked for the day; sometimes it means giving yourself permission to do another thing, instead of remaining splayed out on the carpet like a starfish, lamenting the thing you haven't done. Sometimes it's simply reminding yourself that it's okay to be higgledy-piggledy, because the way you approach your day is your own and nobody else's.

How we can find our own way

- We can compose the day for ourselves, bucking the rigidity of routine in favour of being open to its ebb and flow.

- We might make checklists for our days or weeks, and allow them to be order-less reminders of what makes a good day.

- We might bookend the day with a way to begin and a way to end, creating a container for the muddle in the middle.

- We might alternate between early starts and sleep-ins, allowing our body to rest when it needs to, rather than be rattled by a too-early alarm.

- We might sometimes get to bed early to read, or at other times stay up late watching a new series, letting our interests or whims guide us.

- We might set aside an untouchable day each month to do something that fulfils us, or create a pocket in the day just for that.

- We might play dominoes with our day, and find the starting piece that effortlessly knocks the others over with momentum.

- We might create a weekly rhythm for the different things in our lives, where we worry less about doing everything each day and instead look at the cumulative across several.

- We might embrace setting our own schedule if we are a free-lancer, retiree or business owner, and explore the ways we can pattern our own day rather than feel narrowed by conventional work hours.

- We might block out a night each week in our calendar to make solitude a recurring event.

- We can compose our own days in our own way, without feeling guilty if they don't look like somebody else's—or even like what we expected this morning.

- We can create some buffer room for our human fallibility. Leave the page blank. Let some air in and see what shape it takes. We can accept that we aren't doing the thing today and do the other thing instead. We can learn to embrace the higgledy-piggledy, and let our days unfold in front of us without judgement.

- We can throw away the draft for the ideal routine, and instead meet tomorrow anew. As Ralph Waldo Emerson put it in a letter to his daughter Ellen: 'Finish every day and be done with it. You have done what you could. Some blunders and absurdities no doubt crept in; forget them as soon as you can. Tomorrow is a new day; begin it well and serenely, and with too high a spirit to be encumbered with your old nonsense. This new day is too dear, with its hopes and invitations, to waste a moment on the yesterdays.'

4

The Worry of Wasted Time

I can never understand why I should eat at one or sleep at eleven, if it is, as it often is, my one and my eleven and nobody else's. For, as between the clock and me alone, one and eleven and all other o'clocks are mine and I am not theirs. But I have known men and women living in hotels who would interrupt a sunset to go to dine, or wave away the stars in their courses to go to sleep, merely because the hour had struck.

Zona Gale, *Friendship Village Love Stories*

Time. We can never find enough of it, or we're not doing enough with it. Yet try as we may to pin our to-dos and agendas to each hour the clock shows, it has a way of slipping by. As the Roman emperor and philosopher Marcus Aurelius said, 'Time is like a river made up of things which happen, and its current is strong; no sooner does anything appear than it is carried away, and another comes in its place, and will be carried away too.'

Despite the 24 uniform hours clock-time offers each day, the experience of time passing often feels far more inconsistent—one hour can feel so impactful and filled to the brim, another can be frittered away. Time is not evenly distributed in its perceived worth—the minutes tend to stretch when we're waiting to meet a new lover, but feel snatched from us when we are rushing somewhere and are already late. Some days feel as if they hold the world; others feel like they're empty.

Time feels slippery in part because our perception of time changes. Time itself is a measure of change. It is not passing by us; we are passing by it, comparing the moment before and the moment after. We can perceive time either prospectively, while an experience is happening, or retrospectively, but time also varies depending on how we feel about an experience. Time flies when we are having fun in the moment, but our memories of such novel experiences can make them seem longer, because there is more to look back on. The journalist and author of *Time Warped: Unlocking the Mysteries of Time Perception*, Claudia Hammond, has called this the 'holiday paradox', referring to how time seems to pass more quickly when we are on vacation, but when we return, we often feel like we've been away for ages. In other words, the greater number of new memories we create, the longer an experience—a day—will seem in hindsight. This also accounts for why time seems to pass more quickly as we get older, because we tend to have fewer novel experiences and learn fewer new skills. This again makes a case for variety over routine: we don't want a string of Groundhog Days, we want surprises, possibilities, new experiences, so we have more to look back on.

Even if we recognise time is slippery, a question remains: how do we fill it well? Perhaps by not thrashing around, trying to keep up with the currents of time, and instead being in the flow of the river we're in. As the Romanian philosopher Emil Cioran said in *The Trouble with Being Born*, 'I do nothing, granted. But I see the hours pass—which is better than trying to fill them.'

Perhaps, instead of filling time, we can inspect whether what we fill it with creates a sense of *fulfilment*. It's not that we don't have enough hours in the day for what's on our to-do list—although that can certainly be the case, of course—but rather we don't inspect what's *on* the to-do list often enough, or question what goes on it in the first place. If 'time is how you spend your love', as Zadie Smith wrote in *On Beauty*, then perhaps it's worth asking how we can manage our love, rather than our time.

Time is slippery, and so are we. Many of us have an ever-growing list of things we'd *love* to do when we find the time. Yet despite our best intentions, the list of things we *need* to do is forever outpacing us—commuting, running errands, exercising, shopping for groceries, seeing friends, raising children, getting enough sleep, navigating schedules. Even striving for balance and self-care has become a to-do item. We perpetually delay the things that might fulfil us most because we fill our time with other things, sometimes out of necessity but sometimes because we're afraid to spend our time—our love—in our own way. We may even fill our days with things we dislike—again, sometimes out of necessity to keep our jobs, but sometimes because doing something we love can be difficult or daunting. It requires figuring out what it is we love—and then finding the courage to pursue it. So we move the fulfilling thing to tomorrow, to next week, to when things settle down a bit. We wait for when we will have more time, only for more time to evade us. Even when a swathe of time avails itself to us—say, an entire morning, a weekend, a string of weeks—chances are we'll squander that time through lethargy, indecision or because our slippery selves follow us wherever we go. As the Tasmanian smallholder, restaurateur and food activist Matthew Evans pointed out to me, 'We are still the same people, even with more time on our hands.'

But what if, instead of waiting until we have more time, we just use the time we have? Sometimes I cannot begin a thing until I can see a clear run of time ahead—a clever trick I've learned to delay getting started. I might have some spare time in the morning, but because I have a meeting at lunch, I'll convince myself I cannot begin until that meeting is over. While we are waiting for the perfect swathe of time to arrive, we miss the time we do have for the fulfilling thing—and postpone the enlivening act of doing things for ourselves.

Seizing the splodge in front of you

So how do we make time for the fulfilling thing, rather than just filling our time? One approach is to recognise that time is not something we find—it's a slippery thing we often have to grasp. That is, we have to ask ourselves from moment to moment what we want to be doing. Perhaps once more we have to learn to occupy our time—to live in it—rather than optimise it. Occupying our time requires that we take it for ourselves. While the rhetoric of 'it's all up to you' overlooks that structural inequalities require structural solutions, perhaps we can find some agency in contemplating what is within our control.

Scattered throughout our days are things that grasp our time—an email, an emergency, a task taking longer than we thought—whether we'd like them to or not. This can be frustrating, but also shows that there is some wiggle room. Maybe we can learn how to take our time in small pockets for the things that fulfil us, rather than various interruptions always taking time away from us. The doctor and author Leah Kaminsky doesn't make time for writing, but grabs it whenever she can. 'I have been known to finish the final edits of a book with the toilet lid down and the bathroom door locked just to get a little "quiet time",' she told me.

There's one caveat to this attempt to swiftly grab time: as soon as we think we have it, it slips from our grasp. With that in mind, perhaps it's worth finding a more malleable representation of time than that which a clock provides. I'm fond of the author Robert Dessaix's description of time as a 'splodge'. As he wrote in his memoir *What Days Are For*, 'A liberating way to view time, I find, is as splodges lying in clusters all around me. Instead of hopping obediently from link to link along a chain towards extinction, I pause in a puddle of it here and wallow in a pool of it there.'

Splodge-time, as I now think of it, teaches us to become more comfortable with the shapelessness of time—how it spills out in all directions. Indeed, that might be the beauty of it. Splodge-time is imperfect, rough around the edges, just as we are.

We can also learn to embrace imperfect schedules with splodge-time. I have a habit of telling myself that I can only do certain things at certain times—when in reality, twenty minutes' journalling in the morning can easily become twenty minutes in the afternoon. I've learned the day will always pull us in different directions, so rather than waiting for the perfect moment to get something done, or for an unlikely runway of time to be available, you can seize the splodge you have in front of you.

It can be tempting, when we have a spare 30 minutes, to convince ourselves that it's not enough time to do something, but this ignores the benefits of just making a start. Beci Orpin is a prolific artist, designer and author who is often asked, 'How do you fit it all in?' When I put this question to Beci, her answer was that she has become practised at getting a lot done in a short period of time: she seizes the splodge in front of her, regardless of how long that might be.

To circumvent my habit to delay, I'll set a timer for two minutes and start the activity, telling myself that I can at least do something for two minutes. Often a short burst of focus spills out into more. It's a small exercise in reminding myself that there will never be a perfect time, so we may as well take this time now, even if it's just a couple of minutes.

Telling ourselves we'll just do this thing for the next two minutes or half an hour can also help make a task less daunting. It can be a comfort to think small—to postpone the big thing for the moment, and just do something with the minutes in front of you. But it's also a way of stopping things from piling up. The two-minute rule coined by David Allen in *Getting Things Done* suggests that if there were a task that would take under two minutes to complete, we should just do it now rather than putting it on a list for later.

I DIDN'T DO THE THING TODAY

Not only can we get something done in the same time it might take to plan to do it later, but we also don't have the task weighing on our minds for the rest of the day—or we avoid something bothering us for six months that might take just ten minutes.

This isn't to say that we must optimise every moment and seize every two minutes for work, but rather that we don't have to wait for the perfect moment to arrive to do the fulfilling thing, or even just that pesky admin thing. Naturally, there are times when we need to structure our time in advance, especially to ensure we are respectful of other people's time. Alongside such commitments, we can also recognise when time boundaries are flexible and use what we have at our disposal.

Rather than waiting for the perfect swathe of time to arrive, we can also carve it out for ourselves—we can be time-greedy, even, and designate pockets for the things we want to do. Early in her career as a writer, the now entrepreneur and author Zoë Foster Blake would reserve Saturday mornings to focus on writing books. To protect the morning, she'd spend Friday night in so she could rise early on Saturday and write. Such an approach often means forgoing time for something else—whether it's a dinner with friends or sleeping in on a Saturday morning. What each of us is willing to forgo is, naturally, personal and circumstantial. Perhaps this is where most time-management advice fails us: it ignores that we all have different responsibilities in our days, and what's fulfilling varies from person to person, and from day to day. Zoë's example also shows that setting aside a pocket of time for a specific activity doesn't have to be forever—Saturday mornings are now spent with her family. 'I worked really hard back then,' she told me, 'and I'm glad I did because by the time I got to my thirties, things kind of fell into place.'

The beauty of such designated pockets of time is that they, too, can be flexible. As the artist Peter Drew reminded me, 'I don't think it really matters if I get that quiet time early in the morning or really late at night, but you've got to get it somewhere.'

Maybe this more malleable approach to time can help us take it when we can get it. Or we might see that it's not always that we're running out of time and need to find more of it, but that we're not protecting the time we already have within our grasp. So seize, grasp and be greedy from time to time—the fulfilling thing will thank you.

The time we waste worrying about wasted time

The notion that time is our most precious resource can bring with it a sense of time-pressure. Time is money, we are always told, and time is running out—so we must manage it well and spend it accordingly. We take time-management courses, adopt various techniques, buy new planners, download the latest productivity app, divide our day into blocks so our time is never wasted. Yet in our zealous attempts to account for every hour, we can become more susceptible to wasted-time-worry, the impatient judge that tells us we should be doing more with our time—or doing something else. We can spend an afternoon lamenting the time we wasted that morning, spoiling hours that would otherwise have been available to us.

Sometimes it's not just the hours we worry about wasting, but the scraps of time that get lost in between—the countless minutes spent on bitsy chores, answering emails, replying to texts, waiting for other people. 'Time confetti', a term coined by the director of the Better Life Lab at New America, Brigid Schulte, describes how time is scattered about our days, resulting in the minutes spent on seemingly insignificant actions adding up to a multicoloured mound of 'wasted time'.

To collect our time confetti, we're often advised to adopt time-management techniques such as putting our devices away or bundling similar tasks together. These approaches can prove helpful, especially in reducing the feeling that we're overwhelmed by the pile-up, but they don't address the worry we attach to wasted time, which can compound: when we worry about wasting time, we end up wasting our time worrying.

While time-management techniques might offer us a semblance of control, they often overlook the fact that we aren't vacuums designed to suction every discretionary minute in our day; we are human beings, with varying rhythms, living in fragmented days.

Perhaps we need to shift away from trying to maximise our time and instead try to reduce our worry about wasting it. After all, isn't the surest way of squandering time to worry about wasting it?

Often, when we worry about wasting time, we are comparing ourselves to how productive we assume other people are. But I have a suspicion that most people are 'wasting' more time than they let on. People often hide that they are time wasters, which perpetuates the sense each of us feels that everyone is using their time well, except us. I'm always quietly delighted when I hear admissions from those I interview that they're time wasters too. I remember speaking to the engineer, author and activist Yassmin Abdel-Magied about her tendency to 'waste time' by binge-watching YouTube videos and *The Daily Show*, or doing things that are nice to do but not necessarily required. 'I might have all these things to do on a given day, but if the sun is shining, I'll convince myself it is imperative that I make use of the sunshine,' she told me, then added with a smile, 'But that's living, right?'

We are bound to waste time—we put things off, take too long to start, become distracted, overlook the efficient route, run late, scroll, chitchat too long with a colleague at lunch. But we also judge how we spend our time rather harshly, treating everything that isn't deemed a productive use of our time as a waste, when there may be value in those moments too. As Antoine de Saint-Exupéry wrote in *The Little Prince*: 'It is the time you have wasted for your rose that makes your rose so important.'

We don't have to view every moment we don't spend the way we expected to as a waste—we can simply appreciate the part it played in our life. In a society that emphasises the productive use of time, we can easily forget that time we enjoyed wasting is not wasted time.

And what a pity it is when we don't even start something because we fear it will be a waste of time—for example, we never begin writing our novel because we worry it will never get published, or we don't start learning a language because we expect we'll never visit the country where it's spoken. *What if it's a waste of time?* This may explain why it can be easier to disappear into busy schedules—surely 'wasting' the day on things that fill the time is more acceptable than wasting the day on something that might lead nowhere. But is spending all our time on things that aren't fulfilling really a good use of our limited days? Perhaps it's better to do something we want to do, even if it fails? Surely it's better at least to try than to let time pass us by.

Even the notion of time passing us by can fling us into worry about all the time we've let pass by. What has been helpful for me in such moments is to remember that time cannot be wasted in advance—a sentiment I've borrowed from Arnold Bennett. In *How to Live on 24 Hours a Day*, Bennett writes: 'The next year, the next day, the next hour are lying ready for you, as perfect, as unspoilt, as if you had never wasted or misapplied a single moment in all your career . . . You can turn over a new leaf every hour if you choose.'

So you've spent a few hours worrying rather than beginning something? Turn over a new leaf. You got stuck in traffic and are late to an event? Turn over a new leaf. You had one too many drinks last night and slept for half the day? Turn over a new leaf.

Part of turning over a new leaf, I think, is to recognise that none of us seize every moment—and maybe there is less for us to seize than we tell ourselves. We can add so much to our to-do lists, but there are only so many imperfect splodges in the day. The increasing length of the working day, or the expectations surrounding it, have influenced how much we think we should be working. Anything that's not work can be seen as a waste, which can see menial tasks pile up to the point of overwhelm, or we debate internally whether or not the fulfilling thing is worth pursuing.

But speaking with hundreds of creatives about their days has helped me adjust my expectations around what constitutes a productive working day when the focus is on mostly cognitive tasks. Many of the interviewees mimicked what we find in the daily routines of great artists throughout history, as well as research on knowledge workers: on most days, three to four hours of high-quality, focused mental work is about our maximum. Working beyond that can be a waste.

I learned that time doesn't have to be the measure of quality work. The illustrator Chaz Hutton, known for his cartoons on sticky notes, told me that when he worked nine-to-five he found it frustrating that you could have completed your work for the day, but you'd have to keep 'working' until it was clock-off time. When he transitioned to working as a freelancer, he switched from this time-based measure to a task-based measure, where he would draw on at least three sticky notes a day.

While few of us may make a living from our art, this lesson on defining what is 'enough' is something we can all borrow. Whether that's prioritising the tasks that ensure you're not holding someone up, or putting a limit to the number of emails you respond to in a day, or acknowledging that there's always more work to be done and today you've done enough. On the other side of the coin, sometimes getting the majority of our work done in less time—say, because we are practised in a certain skill—shouldn't mean that the remaining hours are then spent on more work. I've often wondered what all the time-optimising hacks are really for—if we optimise in order to gain more time, then why do we feel guilty or rush to fill that time when we finally get it?

Writer Derek Thompson made a similar point in an essay for *The Atlantic*, 'Three Theories for Why You Have No Time'. Inspecting the decades since the introduction of labour-saving technologies and appliances, Thompson noted that we don't now have more free time on our hands. 'Americans tend to use new productivity and technology to buy a better life rather than to enjoy more downtime in inferior conditions. And when material concerns are mostly met, Americans fixate on their status and class, and that of their children, and work tirelessly to preserve and grow it.'

We don't need every hour to be optimised to accomplish things. Instead, we can simply have more space for *the work of the day*— and the empty time we need in between. Often our encounters with empty time can fling us into boredom, panic or anxiety, or add to our wasted-time-worry. But we need some hours in the day to waste as we wish—just like the negative space in design cushions the text to make it more readable. We need cushioning in our days too.

We can give ourselves space to waste time. We can arrive somewhere early, and sit and look around instead of answering emails on our phone. We can become more comfortable with empty moments rather than rushing to optimise every second. We can enjoy that unexpected phone call from a friend. We can allow ourselves to pause and think. We can see our commuting time as a chance to let our mind wander, rather than scrolling social media. We might achieve a little less, but we'll likely feel a little more centred. By adding some cushioning, we can take our time.

The paradox may be that when we have time, we long for something to fill it with; when it's too full, we long for empty time. I'm familiar with this swing—there are times I relish having nothing to do, and other moments when I miss the scent of plans. It's perhaps by embracing both that we can start to diminish the worry or judgement that each alone can bring.

We will inevitably get lost in Twitter spirals. We will make endless cups of tea. We will be distracted by sunny days, and feel blue on rainy nights. We will find it difficult to define enough. Instead of berating ourselves for the moments we waste, we can value the cushioning they provide—and perhaps even come to appreciate the colourful specks of confetti on our living room floor.

Trust the timing of your life

It's easy to be judgemental about how long a thing takes—we label the space between an idea and action as laziness, as procrastination or as wasting time, when more often than not we're simply not ready yet.

I remember a talk Miranda July gave in which she spoke about being patient with time. It was called 'Lost Child!' and detailed her journey from fledgling artist in Portland to award-winning film-maker and bestselling author. She shared the inner thoughts that ran through her mind on challenging days: *I feel wrong . . . I'm a bad person . . . I barely did anything today, and the one thing I did was bad.*

Most of us have similar thoughts, but July reframed things in a way that has stuck with me: every supposedly useless day, every supposedly useless hour, she said, can still be valuable. It can be valuable thinking time, akin to putting savings away in the bank that will accrue and be there to withdraw when you're ready. As July said, the 'useless' days can be preparation: 'You can't do it today, you are just not smart enough, you have to accrue more time before you suddenly have the whole idea. That is how it is for me—it's a whole lot of misery but these days I just think, well, great, another miserable day in the bank.'

We're quick to label preparation as procrastination, and easily overlook that things take the time they take. Some days we may only spend an hour doing the thing, but it can take all day to set ourselves up for that one potent hour. The time we spend thinking about doing the work can be a necessary part of the process of doing it.

We can also recognise when the circumstances of our lives mean that we have less time to dedicate to the fulfilling thing. We might be quick to label ourselves lazy because we don't dedicate the weekend to doing the thing or working on a side hustle, without realising that we are simply exhausted. We can forget that things take a long time to do—and everyone comes at something from a different starting point. Often the most fulfilling things need more time and space around them—and we need to accrue more knowledge, energy or creativity in order to do them well. As the musician Nick Cave wrote in an advice column for his newsletter, 'The Red Hand Files', to someone who was struggling with a bout of creative block, 'The thing you must hold on to through these difficult periods, as hard as it may be, is this—when something's not coming, it's coming. It took me many years to learn this, and to this day I have trouble remembering it.' Sometimes what can look like a block is just a work process. Things are always on the way to us, even if they haven't yet arrived—we can be patient with the time this expedition can take, in the knowledge that we will be better placed to receive them when we are more prepared.

When something rolls over to the next day's to-do list again and again, there may be a reason. I've seen this in my own projects—there have been times when I've found myself putting something off like starting a podcast or writing a book proposal, and berating myself for not doing it week after week. It's only when I've stopped pushing for something to be done, when I've taken it off my to-do list and let it take the time it takes, that the insight and knowledge I needed arrived on its own timeline. In almost all instances, this loosened grip on a thing and patience towards it has made the doing of the thing far less strained.

That said, I often wonder how to tell the difference between the self-sabotage of perpetually putting things off—which I have been wont to do—and being patient. Asking this question again and again has revealed patterns: when it's self-sabotage, I find myself not doing anything at all, because I'm not doing the thing I *ought* to do. When it's patience, I can turn to another thing and trust there will be a right time to return to something. I remind myself of what the writer and artist Marieke Hardy told me she's come to learn: 'If the creativity is not coming to you for a project, then do something else and trust that it will get done another time.'

The point, I think, is that not everything happens all at once. Sometimes we simply need to turn to something else if we find ourselves stuck. The little things we do around the doing of something can still move a project forward, just not always in the way or on the schedule we had estimated. We should remember 'Hofstadter's law', coined by the author Douglas Hofstadter: things always take longer than you expect, even when you take into account Hofstadter's law.

We do ourselves a disservice when we try to rush what can't be rushed. 'Precrastination', for example, is the inclination to complete tasks quickly for the sake of getting things done, and can be more costly than procrastination as it results in unnecessary effort that with better planning might have been avoided. In other words, haste makes waste—eventually wasting us. Arnold Bennett wrote of 'the danger of developing a policy of rushing, of being gradually more and more obsessed by what one has to do next. In this way, one may come to exist as in a prison, and one's life may cease to be one's own.'

There is an immense pressure to do things quickly and be an overnight success, but if we're too rushed in our days to experience them, what's the point? Why are we rushing to finish something, just to have nothing on the other side of it? The early-twentieth-century radio and film star Will Rogers once wrote, in a letter to *The New York Times*, 'Half our life is spent trying to find something to do with the time we have rushed through life trying to save.'

Perhaps we can favour doing things more slowly and with more consideration. We can put less on our to-do lists so we don't entrap ourselves with more to rush through. We can do another thing if one thing isn't ready yet. Instead of pursuing instant success, we can take our time with the fulfilling things. As I learned from the designer Debbie Millman, anything worthwhile takes a long time.

We must be willing to work at things that are worthwhile for a long time, and often without the perks of instant gratification. In doing so, we become more familiar with the length of time it takes to do worthwhile things—and with how everything has its own pace. As Henry David Thoreau wrote in his journals, 'Consider the turtle. Perchance you have worried yourself, despaired of the world, meditated the end of life, and all things seemed rushing to destruction; but nature has steadily and serenely advanced with a turtle's pace. Has not the tortoise also learned the true value of time?'

'Considering the turtle' means that we can not only be more patient with time, but perhaps also more realistic about what we expect from the hours in our day. According to productivity and time-management expert Julie Morgenstern, there are time realists and time optimists. I am a time optimist: I tend to overcrowd my schedule in the naive hope that I can achieve all of it in a day. There are always reams of things I want to do, and I convince myself that everything is achievable right now. But the antidote to cramming your to-do list is to be a time realist—that is, really looking at a task and breaking down how long it will take. To become a time realist, I have begun to practise setting a yardstick first. For a project or task, I see how much I can progress in a 45-minute block, and then allow that to guide the schedule, rather than setting myself up to fail with an overly optimistic schedule that has no grounding in what is actually achievable. The more we watch what can be done in one hour, the more realistic we will be when planning for the next one.

In learning to become a time realist, I've also recognised the futility of obsessing over the timeline of our lives. Some things take a succession of days, years, even lifetimes to be ready. In *Your Own Kind of Girl*, Clare Bowditch remembered how at 21 she made herself a promise: she would one day write a book. She allowed herself one particularly comforting condition, however: she would wait until she was in her forties to do it. Adding this concession helped Bowditch shut down the cycle of rumination and self-doubt that can accompany our ambitions—the promise created a sense of patience as well as a commitment to the dream. 'I needed the hope of the promise,' she wrote, 'but what I didn't need was the pressure of rushing it.' We can't do everything all at once—but as Bowditch shows, we can do some things at different times, and cultivate patience for the timing of things.

A soft promise rather than rushing through is what can build patience and help us favour timelessness rather than timeliness. In an essay titled 'Navigating Stuckness', the artist and computer scientist Jonathan Harris wrote, 'In the trade-off between timeliness and timelessness, choose the latter. The zeitgeist rewards timeliness, but your soul rewards timelessness. Work on things that will last.'

It's not just the things we want to do that benefit when we favour timelessness, but even our everyday experiences. As I learned from the Australian kids' cartoon *Bluey*, rather than make good time, make good times.

We often ask ourselves where the time goes, and no one really knows. But for things to be worthwhile, for making good times, for things to be timeless, we have to allow them to take the time they take. This doesn't mean that we have to make them perfect, or wait for the perfect moment, or be perfectly optimised. The fruits of our labour might not reveal themselves in a day—some days it can look like we didn't do anything at all—but the knowledge we put in the bank is priceless. So trust the timing of things—trust the timing of your life.

5

The Shifting Goalposts of Ambition

*Desire makes everything blossom; possession
makes everything wither and fade.*

Marcel Proust, *Les plaisirs et les jours*

Days can be dotted with ambitious plots to aim higher, work harder, do more to realise the aspirations we have set for ourselves. A companion to what can at times feel like an exhausting ascent can be a haunting worry about whether we'll ever make it. *Will it work out for me? Will the life I've dreamed for myself ever be within reach? Will I ever get what I desire?*

Perhaps, through our ambitious pursuits, we are trying to prove to ourselves that we're somehow significant—that we are *somebody*, doing *something*, going *somewhere*.

This pressure surrounds us. The steady rise of individualism in Western culture has come with the pursuit of greatness, personal growth and subsequent achievement—not just to be somebody, but to be *somebody special*. From the moment we received that first gold star for our efforts—or didn't—we've internalised the idea that if you make it, you matter. So many of us work hard to keep winning proverbial gold stars from our bosses, partners, friends, industries or communities. Accolades, praise, impressive clients, bigger salaries, material possessions and status have become the markers of success—the sign that we are somebody.

This desire for recognition might be innate—it's human nature to want the star. As the psychologist Williams James said in *The Principles of Psychology*, 'We are not only gregarious animals, liking to be in sight of our fellows, but we have an innate propensity to get ourselves noticed, and noticed favourably, by our kind.' Perhaps it's not the want to be noticed that's a cause for concern, but the lengths to which we go to achieve this. When we aren't the recipients of whatever we've determined to be the marker of specialness, we can all too often feel empty and unfulfilled. As a counterweight, we add more to our days, making our lives faster and busier in the present in pursuit of success and recognition in the future.

Alongside the pervading societal message that we are what we accomplish, we are also told we will never be enough. No matter how hard we work to prove our somebody-ness, there is always somebody who is more of a somebody than we are. We can never quite be good enough, smart enough, successful enough, beautiful enough, fulfilled enough—because there is no end point to such ambition.

Ambition can create in us an avalanche of dissatisfaction, with ourselves and with our days. By its very definition, it describes a state of being—be it successful, wealthy or famous—that we don't yet possess. Instead of finding fulfilment in what we currently have, we are entranced by the allure of what we *could* have—or what's next.

To lack ambition is often regarded as a flaw in character—a sign of complacency or timidity. But I've come to see that it's often our ambition, rather than our lack of it, that can perpetuate disappointment. Ambition can convince us that we can play every part, strive for every accolade, pursue every coveted opportunity. But this can come at a cost: we forgo what we enjoy for something we deem more noteworthy. Instead of taking a moment to uncover what we really want, we keep up a pace that helps us maintain the appearance of success, hurtling towards an image of ourselves or the shadow of someone else, but in doing so drift further and further away from what we really want to be doing.

When we do know what we want or desire, perhaps it still behoves us to learn how to hold a specific ambition in a way that doesn't impede how we define ourselves. I'm reminded of a *60 Minutes* interview Oprah Winfrey gave in 1986. She told host Mike Wallace that she believed *The Oprah Winfrey Show* would do well, to which he asked, 'And what if it doesn't?' Oprah explained that she would still do well because she was not defined by a show. 'It would be wonderful to be acclaimed as this talk show host who has made it, that would be wonderful, but if that doesn't happen there are other important things in my life.'

Perhaps what we call 'ambition' is too narrow because it doesn't always include the myriad important things in our lives. It's often tied to success, growth, more, better, higher. But we can be creative in how we define the concept, and apply ambition to things in our lives beyond work.

Ambitions vary from person to person, and what one might see as unambitious can be ambitious for another. We might reject a promotion to a leadership position because we know our passion lies in the work we already do, rather than in managing other people. We might not take on another demanding freelance client because we'd rather have more time for a creative pursuit. In these examples there is still ambition, but it's not one that is tied to the fame, fortune or recognition we generally associate with the term. In fact, such ambition is far more all-encompassing: it's personal, and it favours going deeper rather than aiming higher.

Even if this more creative definition of ambition resonates deeply, we can still be hesitant to apply it to our own life. We can remain stuck in the traditional trappings of success: a steady job, a house, a partner, a family, a retirement plan. Such ambitions feel safe, almost guaranteed. Or we might see a person we admire and think that we want a life, a career, a partner, a home, a project like theirs. Out of comparison, we set such goals as our ambition, overlooking how different from us someone may be in temperament, interests or circumstances.

Often, when we inspect these cloned ambitions, we find that they are empty wells: they fail to bring us fulfilment. We can place a lot of emphasis on attaining goals that don't really fit us—perhaps making more money, working at a certain company, climbing the ladder. But when we get the paycheque, the dream job, the promotion, we don't feel the sense of contentment we expected.

In such striving, we might think we are working towards finding happiness, fulfilment and meaning, but it's possible we are confusing wanting to be happy with wanting to be satisfied. According to cognitive psychologist Daniel Kahneman, happiness and satisfaction are distinct concepts: where happiness is a spontaneous, fleeting experience, satisfaction is a long-term feeling built over time and based on achieving goals and building upon ambitions.

This often requires a trade-off. Working to fulfil our ambitions—or maximising our satisfaction long term—can undermine our experiences of everyday happiness. As an example, we might recognise that some of our most enjoyable moments include spending time with friends, yet often, when we are focused on a long-term ambition, we are too busy to prioritise socialising. This reminds me of the longest research on happiness, the Harvard Study of Adult Development, where the most important contributor to happiness was found to have nothing to do with wealth or fame, or with working harder and harder. As the director of the study, psychiatrist Robert Waldinger, said, 'The clearest message we get from this 75-year study is this: Good relationships keep us happier and healthier. Period.'

We know good relationships are ultimately more fulfilling than success, yet we sideline our social lives in order to work harder. Of course, there will be times when we want to focus on satisfaction over day-to-day happiness, and need to shuffle our lives in order to focus on a particular goal. I'm reminded of Kenneth Koch's poem 'You Want a Social Life, with Friends', which speaks to how we long for a social life, a passionate love affair and fulfilling work, yet we must face the fact that it may be possible to have two simultaneously, but never three. Maybe two out of three ain't bad.

When an ambition is one of our very own, perhaps the temporary sacrifice feels worth it. But if we're simply striving for the sake of striving, our narrow ambitions can become a block to the life we actually want. We make our days busier in the hope we will one day be recognised for our efforts, all the while leaving ourselves with less time for the things we really want to do, or the people we want to spend time with. Maybe we can find satisfaction not only in our accomplishments, but in the drive that lies behind them. The distinction made by actor and director John Malkovich—in an interview with *GQ* titled 'John Malkovich Has a Secret for Being Insanely Productive'—has always stuck with me: 'Accomplishment may be the result of ambition or drive. And I think I probably have lots of drive. But I don't have any ambition. I never really had any. I don't have a hugely high opinion of ambition. I think of ambition as the need to prove something to others, and the need to be recognized. A need for rewards outside of the work. Drive motivates you to do whatever it is you're doing as well as you can.'

Whereas ambition fixates on external recognition—that proverbial gold star—drive is rooted in what we do and how we do it. It's not about reaching the top in competition with those around us; it's about doing our best. I'm reminded of my conversation with the storyteller Luke Currie-Richardson. When I asked what drives him, he said it was to be the best, but not in the way we usually mean that: 'I don't need to be the best against anybody else; I don't need to be the best for anybody but myself, and give it my all.'

While satisfaction in our ambitions is contingent on them being fulfilled, drive brings a satisfaction in taking the steps towards something—*in doing our best*. Drive is also something we control. We can't guarantee the outcomes of our ambitious striving, but we take our drive with us wherever we go. This differs from 'being driven', I think. Being driven has a target, whereas our drive doesn't go away when we finish something, fail or experience rejection—it continues to propel us. I'm reminded of a conversation I had with Yassmin Abdel-Magied, about how the fear of losing it all can follow us—even when we've already experienced success, opportunities and accolades. 'I once asked my mum, what happens if everything falls apart? What if I lose everything?' she recalled. 'I'll always remember her response: Well, nobody gave you what you've got now. You worked for what you have. So you have to believe that you can work for it again.'

When we see that our drive is within us, we can remember that what we accomplish (or fail to) doesn't have to define us. Toni Morrison wrote an essay for *The New Yorker* called 'The Work You Do, the Person You Are'. In it, she recalled her father's advice after she shared her frustrations about the increasing demands of her cleaning job: 'Listen. You don't live there. You live here. With your people. Go to work. Get your money. And come on home.'

We live in a society that tends to measure our value based on what we do, how hard we work and the results of our actions. But Morrison's reassuring and wise account of this advice reminds us that our value doesn't live in the accolades we receive, or in the number of followers we have on social media—it lives in us. What Morrison heard in her father's advice served as a guide that she summarised as follows, and which provides a useful north star to anyone similarly questioning their work life: '1. Whatever the work is, do it well—not for the boss but for yourself; 2. You make the job; it doesn't make you; 3. Your real life is with us, your family; 4. You are not the work you do; you are the person you are.'

Morrison's fourth observation from the essay speaks to this idea that what we accomplish doesn't define us. Our worth isn't waiting for us to make it, to reach a certain point, to fulfil our dreams— we take it with us wherever we go. We are the ones who make a pursuit or an experience worthwhile; it doesn't make us. What we accomplish doesn't change who we are—we don't suddenly morph into someone special, because there's no such thing. As teacher David McCullough Jr put it in his commencement speech to Wellesley High School in Massachusetts, 'You Are Not Special', 'The sweetest joys of life, then, come only with the recognition that you're not special. Because everyone is.'

When we untangle our worth from what we accomplish, when we uncover a drive that is our very own and not somebody else's, we might just find meaning in doing something that's special to us—or in the act of making it so.

Striving to be micro-ambitious

We needn't do away with ambitions entirely, but perhaps we should frame them in a way that brings more enjoyment to the process instead of judgement.

Perhaps we trip over our ambitions because we fasten them to a desire for instant success. We want applause, recognition, a following almost before we've begun a pursuit. We can easily become intimidated by our own grand schemes of who we will become or what we will achieve, and become discouraged when overnight success doesn't arrive.

While luck and privilege can act as an express lane to fulfilling one's ambitions, there is often a messy, bumpy process behind the veil of success. One of my favourite illustrations by Mari Andrew depicts an iceberg. At the tip is a moment of seemingly spontaneous success, but below the surface is the rejection, the crying, the quitting, the criticism, the late nights and early mornings, the jealousy, and all the putting yourself out there. What I take from this is that we have to find a way to enjoy the subterranean, because that's where we spend the majority of our days. We should savour the efforts behind opportunities, the rejections behind success, the small steps taken along the way.

Even if there were such a thing as being 'somebody special', the only sustainable pathway would be to take things step by step. This is the essence of being *micro-ambitious*, a term I stumbled upon in comedian Tim Minchin's 2013 occasional address to the University of Western Australia. In it he admitted he never had a 'big dream', and instead advocated a passionate dedication to the pursuit of short-term goals: 'Be micro-ambitious. Put your head down and work with pride on whatever is in front of you— you never know where you might end up.' Rather than getting caught up in lofty ambitions, being micro-ambitious plants us in the present so that we pay attention to what we want to achieve today or in this hour. It's about being content with small steps, rather than getting overwhelmed by a big, audacious goal. It focuses on the doing of something, rather than the recognition or reward. When we simply focus on the next small, necessary step, the rest will often follow. As journalist David Carr said in a 2014 commencement address at the University of California Berkeley, 'Don't worry about the plot to take over the world. Just do what is in front of you, and do it well.'

Being micro-ambitious allows us to notice opportunities because we are not rushing ahead or fixated on a narrow outcome. As Minchin put it, we can notice what's on the periphery: 'If you focus too far in front of you, you won't see the shiny thing out the corner of your eye.'

Of course, being micro-ambitious is not to say we should do away with longer-term goals. While empty ambitions narrow our lives, others can expand them—ambitions for community, for the environment, for income equality, for addressing the world's problems. Our aspirations for a better future can be what pulls us out from the discontent of today. The belief that things can be different can propel us forward. We also need ambitious people to tackle societal and environmental issues that seem impossible. The long-term thinking that goes along with ambition is crucial not just for our sense of perseverance, but for future generations. When we live only in the now and think solely of the short term, we suffer: we have overlooked the long term in favour of short-term gains.

Both personal and social ambitions give us something to aim at beyond the short term. They help keep us focused on a goal when the fulfilment of that goal feels far away. One of my favourite sentiments from Neil Gaiman's 2012 commencement speech at the University of the Arts—entitled 'Make Good Art'—frames our ambition as a distant mountain: 'Something that worked for me was imagining that where I wanted to be—an author, primarily of fiction, making good books, making good comics and supporting myself through my words—was a mountain. A distant mountain. My goal. And I knew that as long as I kept walking towards the mountain, I would be all right. And when I truly was not sure what to do, I could stop, and think about whether it was taking me towards or away from the mountain.'

If we know what our mountain is, we can keep it in mind when we need to make choices in our days. In moments of doubt, we can remember the mountain we are steadily walking towards. When we find ourselves surging forward out of comparison, competition or external expectation, we can remember that that's not our mountain.

Our mountain can be used as a guide, but we must remember that we can only take single steps in our walk towards it. When we turn our attention to what's right in front of us rather than what's in the distant future, we might stand a better chance of realising that future anyway: we are moving towards it, rather than being stifled by how far away it seems.

As we inch closer, we must remember that our ambitions sometimes clarify but at other times adapt, because we ourselves are adapting along the way. With each step, the vistas in our periphery change, too. When our desires change, we can course-correct. So don't be afraid to follow whatever catches your eye.

You never arrive

Success can rarely be hurried—even if it arrives quickly, it is often short-lived. As Oscar Wilde wrote in *Lady Windermere's Fan*, there are only two tragedies in life: 'One is not getting what one wants, and the other is getting it.'

Perhaps this trajectory is especially true for our ambitions for success, as they're insatiable. The glimmer that accompanies a reward quickly fades, recognition feels fleeting, and when we get where we wanted to be, we quickly find another place we'd rather be. When I spoke to musician Amanda Palmer, she told me that she related to this. 'The minute you have a modicum of success you want to keep going, keep climbing and keep doing, but it is not sustainable,' she said. This sentiment is one I've felt many times myself, and have heard echoed by the people I've interviewed. Few people ever truly feel like a success, partly because it's an illusion. Psychologists refer to this phenomenon as the 'hedonic treadmill'—the tendency for our brains to adapt to our improved circumstances and search for the next thing that might be improved, without pausing to celebrate our current success or positive change in our circumstances.

This ascent is perpetuated by other people, too. When someone has success in one area, they are asked to do other things: the writer, for instance, is asked to do interviews and give speeches. All the extraneous activities of success draw them away from the very thing that made them successful to begin with.

Then there is society's fixation on 'what's next' after an accomplishment. Instead of reflecting or congratulating ourselves or others on the hard work, we fix our gaze on the next challenge; sometimes we even berate ourselves for not having reached that distant mountain already. There is pressure on us to work faster, harder, to achieve more, and to reach new heights at an increasing pace. Perhaps we need to normalise not knowing what's next—because we never really do.

While we may know on some level that there's no peak of the mountain we will reach when our lives are complete, sometimes we orientate our lives towards the illusion anyway. Throughout our days, we might tell ourselves that life will be better when we get that promotion, leave our job, lose weight, finish this project, win that award—*when we finally arrive.* But the truth is that we never arrive. Not when we get that job, complete that project, find a partner, move into that house, make more money. Because even when we do achieve such things, we are always looking to the next thing, or lamenting the inevitable plateau of a specific ambition.

On the one hand, this can be what propels us forward in life—when we take one step, the next is revealed to us. But on the other hand, we can become caught on an escalator of unfulfilment if we expect to find contentment in the achievement of one goal. So rather than seeing the accomplishment of a particular ambition as the doorway to happiness, we should do away with the idea of a beginning or finishing point entirely, and treat the obstacles as part of the course.

While starting with the end in mind can prove useful in taming our sense of overwhelm, when it comes to our ambitions and goals, it can also exacerbate frustration, disappointment and anxiety because there is no end in sight. The concept of *teleo-anticipation*, a term coined in 1996 by German physiologist Hans-Volkhart Ulmer, suggests that when we can anticipate the end of a task, we stagger our expenditure of energy in order to sustain the doing of that task. But what happens when there is no end, like in our ambitious pursuits? Or when the sense of arrival remains elusive?

In an article for *The Globe and Mail* titled 'COVID-19 Is Like Running a Marathon with No Finish Line', Alex Hutchinson wrote about how 'staying in the moment might be better for us than fantasizing about a future just beyond reach'. Hutchinson pointed to the example of endurance sports, and what happens when you hide the finish line. Researchers have found that the only way to handle not knowing when you'll reach the end is to step into the moment. 'It turns out that, if you ask yourself "Can I keep going?" rather than "Can I make it to the finish?" you're far more likely to answer in the affirmative,' Hutchinson noted. The lesson we can take from this is to resist investing too much in who we will be when we arrive—to dismantle the false promises of happiness, success and completion that we expect to experience if we fulfil our ambitions.

Just because we will never really arrive doesn't mean we can't take a moment to reflect on and celebrate our successes along the way. Sometimes we need to direct our sense of achievement onto our lives right here, and not our ambitions for the future. We can celebrate each step, revelling in the small things; we can also look back and see how far we've come, rather than worry about where we might be going.

It's human nature to keep seeking out the next step—it's what can provide momentum and drive progress—but perhaps we can sometimes take a moment to survey the view from wherever we stand. After all, what happens during the in-between moments of our lives is the very making of our lives. There is no end point to our days while we are living them. Once we arrive at the end of one, we find ourselves at the starting point of another—and what happens in the middle is what we call a life.

So rather than being stuck on the treadmill of the next thing and the next thing, we should be inspired regularly by what we have learned, and reflect on what we could do differently, how we have felt, what we have enjoyed or experienced, and how we have changed.

Ambition itself is not a character flaw—it can guide and propel us. But when we use it to fill our internal sense of emptiness, we run in circles. Instead of asking what ambition, what goal, what achievement will make us special—and make us feel whole—we can keep jostling with the incomplete parts of ourselves. We can stop worrying about how the rest of our lives will turn out, and simply get through the smaller challenges we will encounter today. We live in this day, after all, not in the one we're waiting for.

6

The Myth of Balance

*Our mental life, like a bird's life, seems to be made
of an alternation of flights and perchings.*

William James, 'On Some Omissions of Introspective Psychology'

Balance. It's often described as something missing from our life,
or the key to a good one. We strive for balance between our work,
our health, our relationships, our passions. We put it on our new
year's resolution list, we follow other people's tips on how to find
it, we attempt to partition off parts of our lives in order to protect
it. Until we reach this state of balance, we feel as if we're getting the
days wrong.

Balance, by definition, is the process of achieving or maintaining equilibrium. This can often be interpreted as a simple equation:
when there is too much work, we must add some rest. But what we
overlook when striving for balance is that what's at either end of the

scale isn't like-for-like. As the comedian Jacqueline Novak put it in an episode of the podcast she co-hosts, *POOG*, 'My wellness will not be homogenous; my balance will be the tiny thousand-pound nail on one side of the scale and six thousand grapes on the other.'

How can we expect to find perfect balance when our lives aren't made up of equal counterparts? Not only do the parts of our lives appear different on the proverbial scales, but they are also perpetually shifting. Rarely do our days allow for such precise addition and subtraction—and even if we did find the perfect balance, something else is bound to come along and tip the scale soon enough.

What's perhaps more likely is for the seesaw to wobble as we hop off and on. In fact, to move we must be okay with feeling unsteady. When we resist the wobble, when we try to find perfect balance even though we're in motion, we only intensify the jolt.

Even our mind wobbles and flipflops between confidence and doubt, interests and disinterests, contentment and discontentment; why do we expect balance in our days when we are constantly changing within them? We might ask ourselves and others if we're doing it right, doing too much, doing enough, heading in the wrong direction, or if we've made a mistake. But I've come to realise that we all wobble, we all falter, we are all not quite sure. Interviewing successful creatives about the behind-the-scenes of their daily lives has taught me that no matter how together someone may appear from the outside, they always have doubts, insecurities and uncertainties inside. The person you think is as steady as a lamppost often feels as if they're walking on a trampoline.

What if, instead of striving for balance and stability, we embrace the wobble? Rather than striving for a life of perfect order, we can wobble between those tasks and commitments that are most meaningful, pressing or simply desirable in each moment.

Rather than setting rules primed for balance and perpetually failing, we can wobble between different habits, responsibilities and interests. We can apply self-awareness rather than self-regulation to the things to which we give our time and attention, instead of simply checking boxes. This means we can still identify the things that have proven to steady us—whether that's eating well, meditating, going for a morning swim, getting a coffee from that friendly barista—but we can also acknowledge that these things won't always neatly stack up each day in perfect harmony.

Wobbling is a process of constant adjustment—you can be moving towards equilibrium and acknowledge that you don't necessarily find yourself settled there. It's a dance between diligence and flexibility, adding and subtracting. It's an *act of balancing*, rather than balance itself.

Yet many of us miss moments in our day because we berate the wobble rather than go with it. We're so busy trying to keep the day on track. We're so hard on ourselves for wobbling, even though it's our natural tendency to wobble—to oscillate between perching and taking flight, both in our inner life and the world around us. Balance also overlooks the inherent differences in each experience, each day, even if on the surface they appear similar. As psychologist William James wrote in *The Stream of Consciousness*, 'We take no heed, as a rule, of the different way in which the same things look and sound and smell at different distances and under different circumstances.'

We're bound to be inconsistent, because our daily experiences, emotions and desires are inconsistent. Yet we often confuse intensity with consistency, further muddling this idea of balance. As the author Simon Sinek explained in a talk for RSA Events, there is a distinct difference: 'Intensity is like going to the dentist, it is fixed in time, we know exactly which date we are going, we know how long we are going to be there, and we know when we come out our teeth will feel smooth and look pearly. But if that is all we do, all our teeth will fall out. In other words, intensity is not enough.'

Similarly, just as only going to the dentist may cause our teeth to fall out, if we miss a day or two of brushing our teeth, they are unlikely to fall out. Consistency doesn't have to be perfect; rather, it's an accumulation of what we do over time. As the British novelist and thinker C.S. Lewis supposedly once observed, 'Isn't it funny how day by day nothing changes, but when you look back everything is different?'

Balance is similar—we might feel that we wobble from day to day, but if we take a longer view, we can find that we have been balancing the various parts of our lives all along. We might not read every night before bed, but have stretches of weeks where we devour several books. We might not have a daily regime but rather a weekly rhythm. Sometimes we're plodding away at something, working steadily day by day, and at other times we sprint to the finish line. Life happens in peaks and troughs, and we wobble with it.

That's what really changed this idea of balance for me: seeing consistency as an accumulation over time, not a perfect adherence. I've never been much good at doing things diligently every day, but when I take the long view, I can see the accumulation of my efforts—whether in my exercise habits or my career milestones. The behavioural scientist Michelle Segar, in a podcast interview, said of exercise that we should take any and every opportunity to move, in any way possible, at whatever speed you like and for any amount of time. I think this flexible approach applies to many things—everything counts, even if it's bitsy. Bit by bit, it all adds up.

Besides, the days we might feel most off-kilter might have less to do with whether we did or didn't do the thing in a set way, and more to do with whether we felt we acted in a way that is in alignment with who we are: whether we kept a promise to ourselves, whether we did what we can in the way it was possible, whether we listened to our body—or even followed a whim. Maybe we aren't searching for perfect consistency so much as for congruence—a compatibility with our wobbly selves, and how we approach the balancing act of our days.

When I'm being hard on myself for wobbling, I hop online and watch Kirsten Lepore's animated film *Hi Stranger*. The strange yet delightful character tells me: 'I just want to sit here and relax with you. Wow, look at the sunset. It's so nice to stop and take all this in. It really makes you enjoy being alive.' Suddenly I feel a bit more alive to the day, and to the things happening in it, and less concerned about a particular wobble. The character continues: 'I've been thinking about you a lot lately. I see you trying to do so many things at once. Worrying about a decision you made, or worried that you said the wrong thing to someone. You're so hard on yourself.'

Then my inner monologue takes over: *Do you see? You're so hard on yourself, Madeleine—you're always trying to fix, change, improve, grow, arrive somewhere steady. You're not allowing yourself to wobble, even though you know it's a part of life. Most of all, you're forgetting that everyone around you is wobbling too.*

'You're wonderful,' the character says. 'You're worthy of being loved. You really are. You just have to let yourself believe it.' Thank you, strange and delightful stranger.

Starting small by forgiving our day-to-day wobbles might prepare us for the bigger, more unpredictable knocks that life presents. We can learn to let a wobble just be a wobble, adjust and move on. We can stop being so hard on ourselves for being human—for feeling tired, for skipping meditation, for taking longer to rest and recover. We don't need to let our entire lives reverberate around us because of a wobble. We can continue with our day and take it all in—wobbles and all.

Absorbing and squeezing

As wobblers, we are constantly oscillating between different modes—focus and rest, order and chaos, company and solitude. This doesn't mean to suggest we have to constantly change, but rather that we straddle change and stability as we flutter and falter. We are perpetually breathing in and breathing out, between doing and not doing. Yet we can be quick to judge either side—we aren't doing enough or we are doing too much. Perhaps we need to honour both stages, and those in between.

To embrace the different modes and our energy within them, perhaps we can liken ourselves to a sponge: there is the absorbing and the squeezing. Sometimes you need to do nothing but absorb inspiration, knowledge or find rest, but if you sit and absorb too long, you can become oversaturated and succumb to inertia. So, like a sponge, you also need the squeeze—the doing, the action, the outpouring of ideas. This analogy can buoy us during quiet periods

I DIDN'T DO THE THING TODAY

in our life, encouraging us to remember our need to refill, and during times of busyness, because we know rest will soon follow. Each mode informs the other: the absorb enables the squeeze.

In order to squeeze, of course, you need to have absorbed something in the first instance. Take writer and poet Maxine Beneba Clarke. For her, a lot of writing happens in the absorbing phases, but it took her a long time to learn to give that part of the process enough space—we often fall into the 'if only' spiral and feel guilt, anxiety or shame for not doing enough as we absorb.

Absorbing isn't something to lament or hurry through, but a crucial ingredient for inspiration and restoration. Whether it's writing, problem solving or recharging before a string of social events, when we skip over the absorb phase, it can lead to what Maxine calls 'dead time': 'If I haven't thought enough about something in my head and I haven't conceptualised it enough, what I put on the page is not likely to be brilliant. It's taken me a long time to see there is a strong point in going for a long walk, getting some fresh air, and thinking about how I can write a story.'

Even if we aren't creative professionals, we all ebb and flow with whatever the task at hand might be. When the flow's not coming, it's often a sign we need to do more absorbing—we can put ourselves in the world and be inspired by it.

Productivity guilt, anxiety or shame is a common companion in the absorb phase, as we live in a society that favours the squeeze—the busy, the doing, the having-something-to-show. We've put activity on a pedestal, when thinking is just as important. We typically label absorbing as procrastination, but as we might remember from Miranda July's bank metaphor, it's often that we simply need to accrue more time. Often we don't allow ourselves the time to think because it doesn't count as work—either by our own or by society's definition. But the best ideas don't come from frantic activity; they come from the processing we do beforehand. The absorb phase is where we make novel connections, have flashes of insight.

This is true for all types of endeavour that require us to think conceptually and creatively. When I interviewed the cook and food author Julia Busuttil Nishimura, she mentioned that going to the market is often a full-day event. Sometimes a feeling of anxiety can follow her there because it doesn't feel like 'work', but the market is also where she gets a lot of her inspiration for new recipes, and her interactions with local producers are integral to that. It can be surprising what we judge about our process, but when we reflect on our days we can see that something we may have labelled as inefficient or menial is actually a crucial part of the work.

It's unrealistic to think we can be doing the important or fulfilling thing all the time. Sometimes we need to do a bit more thinking, planning and absorbing to make the juice worth the squeeze. Equally, the squeeze—the radiant action and the times we are in flow—gives what we have absorbed its meaning. It's where we put what we've learned into action, where we turn thinking into writing, study into knowledge, fresh produce into recipes, and solitude into a deeper connection to ourselves and to others.

Just as we need to honour the absorb phase, we also need the well-timed squeeze. It makes sense that we might linger in the absorb phase when we face adversity, uncertainty or exhaustion. We are protecting ourselves. Yet there are also times we become saturated with planning, overthinking and even researching, to the point of inertia. We resist the squeeze we've been preparing for, and forget that some things don't need to be overthought.

Knowing the difference between needing the absorb and needing the squeeze can be like a dance. Sometimes, when I'm stuck and can't figure out what action to take next, I ask myself whether I need to absorb or whether I need to squeeze. For the absorb period, I write down everything on my mental to-do list so I can see it in front of me, and I then analyse it and prune it back to allow myself more space for inspiration.

For times when I need the squeeze, I add things to my calendar. Whether it's a new class, a social catch-up or a business meeting, I want to purposefully crowd my days so that I feel a sense of momentum, or the push to spring into action that comes with not having quite enough time. Busyness when on our own terms can often be motivating, after all. Perhaps counterintuitively, I might even embrace leaving things until the last minute to feel the squeeze—not doing the thing today can light a fire under my feet for tomorrow, when I might have otherwise been complacent.

I've also found that from day to day there can be a pattern of absorbing and squeezing—I'll work in fits and spurts, rather than a set nine-to-five. Some days it feels like I'm firing on all cylinders and a long stretch of work feels effortless, but the next day my engine is sputtering. I'm learning that's part of the process: while some people are more inclined to plod along, my focus is rarely evenly distributed across my days.

Sometimes we can become stuck in one phase—perhaps it's our default setting, or we've become too comfortable with the doing or the not doing. Other times, external circumstances—say, a global pandemic or the need to earn more money—determine whether we are in an absorb or squeeze phase. We might spend years in the absorb phase, or find ourselves in the squeeze for longer than we'd like out of necessity. That's when it's important to remember that life happens in cycles. For some of us, our health and life circumstances can make it difficult to force the squeeze; rather, we need to be okay with the sometimes unpredictable nature of our bodies and minds. In her collection of essays, *Show Me Where It Hurts: Living with Invisible Illness*, the artist and critic Kylie Maslen likened the daily variances of her health conditions to storms—we can't stop them from happening, but we can try to minimise their harm. 'Just as storms have seasons, the triggers that cause me pain or distress come in patterns,' she wrote. 'I can't prevent them; I can only do my best to soothe this particular cycle until it dies out. Then I look around me at the land that has been flattened and destroyed, as if a cyclone has swept across my life. I begin to pick up the pieces and rebuild, but I never lose sight of the sky, knowing the wind can pick up again anytime.'

The length of time we spend absorbing or squeezing can sometimes be out of our control. When we encounter a lull or a quiet period in our career or personal life, we can tend to take the blame, internalise it as a failure or wish to rush through it. But perhaps, as with a storm, nature can assure us that there will be ebb and flow—the winter fallow time, the blossoming of the spring. As an inspirational Pinterest post reminds us, 'If nothing in nature blooms all year, why should you?' Many artists I've interviewed maintain intense work schedules but often only for seasons at a time, because they recognise the importance of each.

I DIDN'T DO THE THING TODAY

As the illustrator Adriana Picker told me, 'The fallow winter is just as important as the bountiful, productive spring.' In our creative practice, our relationships, our calendars and our energy, we can borrow this metaphor of the seasons and apply it to a day, a period of time, or follow the seasons themselves. We can make winter a time for retreat, spring for sowing seeds and finding inspiration, summer for growth and autumn for harvest, before we allow for the leaves to fall once more and find rest. Even if we're not creative practitioners, we can look at our days through the lens of creativity and take the long view: it's the rhythm of seasons, years and decades that teaches us about how we adapt and change and settle into ourselves over time. Recognising when to absorb and when to squeeze means we can capitalise on both the momentum and fulfilment that action can bring, as well as the reflection that space can afford us.

The storm, the seasons, the sponge—all these analogies can help us acknowledge that there is an ebb and flow to our days, and not some perfectly aligned middle point we must find and maintain. We can't be perfectly balanced as we navigate the pendulum swing of our days—we can only wobble towards what we need.

Everything in moderation—including moderation

The key to balance, it is often said, is moderation. But for some of us—myself included—moderation can feel impossible to sustain. Instead of trying to uphold moderation, only to fall into the 'if only' spiral, we can embrace our all-or-nothing tendencies.

Perhaps, for some, it might be easier to do something every day, rather than three times a week. Some people find it easier to abstain totally than to do something moderately—we don't eat just one piece of chocolate because we know we'll eat the whole block. Other times, we want indulgence—sometimes we don't mind if we do eat the entire block of chocolate or stay up until sunrise—we want the sense of rapture that hedonism can bring to our days.

Maybe oscillating between abstaining and indulgence can be our version of balance. We often try to dilute intensity or excess with moderation, but great things can come from being someone who swings to different sides of the pendulum. To borrow from one of the many volumes of *The Diary of Anaïs Nin*, 'Something is always born of excess: great art was born of great terror, great loneliness, great inhibitions, instabilities, and it always balances them.'

The writer and author of *Better Than Before*, Gretchen Rubin, framed this as each of us being either 'abstainers or moderators'. Like the all-or-nothing types, abstainers find it easier to give something up entirely rather than indulge moderately. As she explained, this approach helps lighten the mental load. I can relate—for me, not doing something sometimes requires less self-control than doing something. There's no right way or wrong way, wrote Rubin. 'It's just a matter of knowing which strategy works better for you. If moderators try to abstain, they feel trapped and rebellious. If abstainers try to be moderate, they spend a lot of time justifying why they should go ahead and indulge.'

The issue Rubin pinpointed is that—as with all prescriptive advice around routine, balance and time management—abstainers and moderators often try to convert the other side. Of course, our preference for one or the other can change, but rarely will that happen because of the judgements of other people, or our own self-recriminations.

For the all-or-nothing types, it might be easier to strike out the idea of balance entirely. In his essay 'Laugh, Kookaburra', the writer David Sedaris recalled a car conversation in which his friend asked the passengers to picture a four-burner stove: one burner represents your family, another your friends, the third your health, and the fourth your work. The idea is that 'in order to be successful, you have to cut off one of your burners. And in order to be *really* successful you have to cut off two.' It's a favourite passage of mine, as it speaks to the illusion of balance as well as the trade-offs behind most versions of success. We make the mistake of thinking we aren't doing enough because we don't have all four burners lit, when it's actually very difficult for anyone to sustain them all at once. Life rarely comes at us in moderation.

The four-burner theory also creates room in which we can experiment with various parts of our lives—if we turn off our social life burner, how does that affect the others? Many people lived this situation during the many pandemic lockdowns. No doubt there was loneliness and grief for our social lives, but for some there was also a sense of relief. An empty calendar allowed us to clarify what we miss, or what we wish to protect in the future.

To me, instead of finding perfect balance or adhering to moderation, it's about asking what sets you alight at different times. Which burners we keep on or off is going to change over time, not just because of the demands of our life, but because of the flickering nature of our interests and priorities—and we can learn to adjust the flame accordingly.

Perhaps the burner analogy differs for moderators and abstainers. For the all-or-nothing types, it may suit to have a burner either on or off. For moderators, maybe it's possible to keep everything simmering at once. Or maybe we land somewhere in between, where indulgence can be part of our form of balance. As the musician Ella Hooper told me, 'I'm all and everything, and I somehow fit it all into the one day—the chocolate biscuits and the vegetable soup.' We can make room for the proverbial 'healthy' thing and the 'treat' without judging either.

Our lives are filled with trade-offs—between our work and our social life, our social life and our health. But the strict rules of balance seem to ignore that we can be chaotic in some areas and structured in others. We can feel too lazy and too busy. We can be diligent and slack. We can eat chocolate biscuits and vegetable soup. We can absorb in the morning and squeeze in the afternoon. The most important thing is to remember that we can break the rules we have created for ourselves if they no longer fit.

Our burners are perpetually in flux, whether we've consciously decided to focus on one part of our lives for a period of time, or because of our external circumstances. In any case, perhaps we can all take a longer view when it comes to the trajectory of our lives— and remember that some things are a slow burn.

The richness of variance

Balance is not only elusive, it might also be a rather unsatisfying life goal. When we are balanced, we are stationary, resisting any change, holding our breath as we try to stay still.

Perhaps what keeps us fixated on finding balance is our longing for what we don't have. If we're busy with work, we long for more time to spend with friends. If our life is filled with social plans, we long for an evening to ourselves. When our days feel messy, disorganised, unpredictable, we crave order. When our lives feel monotonous, we long for spontaneity. Our wants contradict, compete and shift. And once we get something, we often wonder what all the fuss was about. A stagnant, perfectly apportioned life rarely provides as much levity as one that swings. As the social researcher Hugh Mackay wrote in *The Inner Self*, 'If we were perfectly rational, we might be able to create a perfectly ordered life, though it would be an excruciatingly dull one.'

We can enjoy the wobble, as it gives our days meaning. And the greater the wobble or swing between intense experiences, the better. As Scott Barry Kaufman wrote in 'In Defense of the Psychologically Rich Life' for *Scientific American*, the most thrilling moments in our lives—the ones that define who we are—often teeter on a knife's edge between pleasure and pain. This is where the key differences between a happy life and a meaningful life are drawn—rather than the emphasis being on whether a given experience is good or bad, it's about the intensity of such experiences. This is because intensity prompts contemplation, which is where we create meaning.

We all know this at some level—that without pain and discomfort, we wouldn't appreciate joy and pleasure, and that we grow from varied experiences. Problems can propel and sustain us as they provide a focus, something to work towards. Yet we are perpetually told to find balance and calm instead of allowing for the swing. Do we want placid, problem-free, balanced days, or do we want to plunge into varied experiences that teach us the most about ourselves and make us feel the most alive?

If variety adds meaning to our lives, then maybe the shifts in our day can have a similar effect. We might search for balance as a comfort to ourselves—life can appear easier with a semblance of predictability—but by narrowing our days, keeping things on an even keel, we miss out on the reflections, lessons and meaning we find in the wobble. Striving for constant stability and productivity limits our freedom to express all that we are and can be—there is an incredible richness in being imbalanced, because that is where we encounter variety.

When I interviewed illustrator Maira Kalman, I learned that we can embrace imbalance. First we ask ourselves what the recipe for balance is, she explained, then we subvert it. 'Once you ask that question, then you can start to see that maybe there is no right balance—there's just a constant change and shift.' It's in this constant variance that we find meaning. 'You can't have the kind of perceptions that you have at 65 when you're 25,' Kalman added, 'and I don't think it would even be good to have that kind of wisdom—it might prevent you from doing all the stupid things that you should be doing.'

We need the moments in our lives that are imperfect and unsteady because it's all part of the story of who we are. As Kalman told me, 'Everything's where it is and it's good. Even the things I'm unhappy about in my life have allowed me to persevere and to be patient. I have all the variations and all the sorrows and all the happiness—and that's my life.'

Perhaps it's not the lack of balance that worries us, but the worry that we've got what's on our individual pair of scales wrong in the eyes of others. But the beauty of cultivating congruence with ourselves—and listening to our own definition of balance, however counterintuitive it may appear to others—is that only we can judge how we wobble between the various aspects of our life. It's impossible to find a formula for balance that suits everyone, because it's impossible to know what's compatible with the circumstances, demands and wants of everyone.

In the film *Princess Cyd*, sixteen-year-old Cyd is in the kitchen with her aunt, Miranda, tidying up after a dinner party. Miranda reaches for a piece of leftover cake for herself and also offers Cyd a slice, to which Cyd replies: 'Maybe if you had more sex, you wouldn't eat so much cake.' The words are accidently cruel, but they also suggest there are rules to the pleasures we add to our lives. What gives meaning or a sense of fulfilment to one person's day might be completely overlooked by another. Yet we see common prescriptions to find this elusive balance all the time—try mindfulness, do a yoga class, eat less cake. We forget that it's not a moral failing to enjoy one pleasure but not another, to have one burner on but not another, to be one way and not another. We can find our own version of fulfilment—from an afternoon spent reading or by having a piece of leftover cake. After all, as Miranda reminds young Cyd: 'We are different shapes and ways and our happiness is unique. There are no rules of balance.'

It's an important reminder not only to reserve self-judgment when we wobble, but to reserve judgement about somebody else's wobble—the notion of balance, enjoyment and how we look after ourselves looks different for everyone. Even more reason to find what works for us. Instead of trying to follow someone else's rules or getting caught up in our own, we can seek things that feel congruent with who we are at this moment in time, and wobble as we discover more. We can allow our days to unfold with curiosity rather than judgement.

Life is movement, not stagnant balance. Enjoy the slice of leftover cake, enjoy the moments by yourself, enjoy the squeeze, enjoy the absorbing, and enjoy the soup and the biscuits. Be all and everything, or all or nothing. Enjoy whatever is your particular way of wobbling through your days, and learn to value the variety.

7

The Standstill of Indecision

The content of your character is your choice. Day by day,
what you choose, what you think and what you
do is who you become.

Heraclitus

Our days are composed of thousands of decisions. Some are seemingly trivial—when to exercise, what to have for dinner, what book to read. Others feel like they define our lives.

What a privilege, what freedom, to have options—and also what a responsibility. If we view our future as a composite of the decisions we make, then we must choose wisely. Perhaps this is what some of us find most difficult about making decisions—the weight we place on them. We can find ourselves in an indecision spiral when we consider how everything hinges on what we decide, or obsess over whether we are making the right call.

All these options, all this weight, can mean we reach a standstill of indecision. How do we do the thing today if we can't decide what that thing is? How do we arrive at a decision when we are faced with a multitude of choices—real or imagined, desirable or undesirable, significant or insignificant, conscious or unconscious? What do we do in those moments when we find ourselves unable to make any decision at all?

Of course, not all decisions are up to us—options vary from person to person, day by day, circumstance by circumstance. But the act of making a decision can be where we languish. A metaphor in *The Bell Jar*, by Sylvia Plath, illustrates this standstill of indecision. The protagonist imagines her life before her like a fig tree, the tip of every branch representing a wonderful future that beckons and winks—relationships, family, careers, travel, athletic pursuits, and many more figs that can't quite be made out from the position she's in. We can find ourselves wanting each and every one of these futures, and when society tells us we can have it all—through advertisements, media or upbringing—perhaps we expect it. Yet in spite of the messaging, we sense that making a decision to pursue one life means forgoing other options. As Plath wrote, 'I wanted each and every one of them, but choosing one meant losing all the rest.' The Latin root of the verb 'decide' literally means 'to cut off'—and in the metaphorical sense 'to kill'. No wonder we hesitate—it can bring a sense of comfort to keep our options alive—we can make a cosy nook out of our indecision where no wrong turn can be made, where all our futures can exist safely and we can rest our head on diaphanous pillows of poss-ibility. But as Plath's fig-tree metaphor shows, we might find out

I DIDN'T DO THE THING TODAY

too late that indecision isn't all that comforting—it's stifling and we risk never reaching for any opportunity: 'I saw myself sitting in the crotch of this fig tree, starving to death,' wrote Plath, 'just because I couldn't make up my mind which of the figs I would choose.' At times we can starve in our hesitation, and other times we can find ourselves gorging on every fig to avoid making the wrong decision or putting an end to a possibility—we take on too much, say yes to every opportunity and find ourselves busy, overwhelmed, exhausted.

Keeping our options open may be the defining characteristic of our time, according to the writer and civic reformer Pete Davis. In his 2018 commencement speech at Harvard University, he described a familiar scenario: 'It's late at night and you start browsing Netflix looking for something to watch. You scroll through different titles—you even read a few reviews—but you just can't commit to watching any given movie. Suddenly it's been 30 minutes and you're still stuck in Infinite Browsing Mode, so you just give up—you're too tired to watch anything now, so you cut your losses and fall asleep.'

Davis went on to discuss what the philosopher Zygmunt Bauman called 'liquid modernity'. 'We never want to commit to any one identity or place or community, so we remain like liquid in a state that can adapt to fit any future shape. Liquid modernity is Infinite Browsing Mode but for everything in our lives.'

Spending our days in Infinite Browsing Mode is akin to sitting in the crotch of the fig tree. We may be rich in possibilities, yet we can find ourselves in a limbo, deprived of the fulfilment that comes from choosing one option and committing to it.

What we often overlook when we delay putting an end to our options is that there's no guarantee we can keep them alive anyway. Eventually, the very options we are contemplating might disappear entirely. Our indecision *is* a decision. Plath concluded: 'As I sat there, unable to decide, the figs began to wrinkle and go black, and, one by one, they plopped to the ground at my feet.'

Recalling this metaphor when I'm in an indecision spiral is sometimes enough to nudge me out of it. Other times, even when I have reached for a metaphorical fig, I can second-guess my decision or find myself wondering whether, if I'd only reached for that other branch, I would be more content with my choice. This is what the American psychologist Barry Schwartz called the paradox of choice—while more choice often brings more individual freedom, not only is it difficult to choose, but even when we do, we can end up less satisfied than if we had fewer options in the beginning. Perhaps the gravest aspect of the indecision standstill is that it is making us miserable. As Schwartz said in a TED Talk titled 'The Paradox of Choice', 'There's no question that some choice is better than none. But it doesn't follow from that that more choice is better than some choice.'

With an abundance of choice, what I often overlook is the privilege of choosing between good options: if all the figs appear plump and ripe, can't I just choose any and trust it will be delicious? Why am I entangled in the relentless pursuit of *better*—sometimes long after a decision has been made?

Changing our minds is something we are programmed to do, especially when our confidence is low about whether a decision is 'right'. As part of a survival-of-the-fittest mentality, we have a tendency to compare opportunities in order to secure the best we can. In this way, contemplating our options can mean we're engaging with our lives—we're keeping things fresh and open to change. Being free of indecision could suggest that we are risk-averse and closed off from the possibility that things could be different—that perhaps we can choose something different for ourselves.

But there's a fine line between being open to possibilities and being overwhelmed by them. When we can change our mind at the last minute with a quick text, our day can become a moveable feast as we heap choice on more choice, to the point that it becomes impossible to digest anything.

What might be preventing us from being content with our choices is something the author and entrepreneur Patrick McGinnis named 'FOBO'—a fear of better options—which leads to stress, dissatisfaction and even regret over our decision. McGinnis told me that FOBO is an 'affliction of affluence', a by-product of our hyper-busy, hyper-connected world where anything is possible. Those experiencing it are, by definition, spoilt for choice.

Unlike another popular term McGinnis coined, 'FOMO'—the fear of missing out—which can teach us more about what we want in life, a fear of better options offers very little benefit. We can find ourselves coveting possibilities that may never be within our reach. That's the thing about options—sometimes the alternatives don't have to exist for us to become stifled by them. Real or imagined, the most toxic part of decision making, McGinnis told me, is going over the same options again and again.

So how do we stop our fear from spinning us around in circles? A piece of advice I once received was to tell myself that

I'm excited rather than nervous—say, before speaking to a room full of strangers. This small flip can be grounding, and I've found the same can be said for my own bouts of FOBO—rather than feeling overwhelmed by options, I can feel excited to have them.

Knowing we have options doesn't have to fling us into a relentless pursuit of better; it can provide excitement or hope. In moments of ennui, reminding myself I have choices often helps imbue me with the resolve I need to take action—I can ask more questions, I can choose a different book to read, I can decide what I want to share or hold back, I can choose whom I spend my time with, I can move cities, I can change jobs. Where a daily practice of gratitude hasn't stuck—for example, the gratitude journal in which I intended to note three things each day to appreciate now just gathers dust—I find these reflections on choice inadvertently bring about gratefulness in me.

In this way, appreciation of our choices can be the very thing to move us out of the indecision spiral. What a privilege, what a freedom it is to have choices—and to embrace the responsibility and act on them. We don't have to obsess about the direction we are going, or the speed at which we're going there—this is, after all, speculation. We can simply settle on a decision and see where it leads.

Perhaps there's also something to be said for choosing to settle into various parts of our days. The illustrator Kim Lam and the philosopher Jason Fox told me about their nightly ritual of 'couch time'—each finds their respective spot on the couch and settles in, free from the gnawing feeling that they should be doing something else or scanning for better options for the evening.

I DIDN'T DO THE THING TODAY

That prompted me to think about the resistance we can have towards this idea of settling. We're told not to settle—we must keep striving, keep extending ourselves. But it can also be recharging, restful and even renewing to simply settle in with no regrets. When we feel settled, we can find space, clarity and focus.

This isn't to say we should settle for less. Rather, we should appreciate that there is meaning to be made in the settling—in arriving at a decision and giving ourselves the opportunity to become comfortable with it. What we settle into doesn't have to be grand—we can settle into a place, a hobby, a plan for the weekend, a community, a regular dinner with friends or family.

Settling helps us live well with the foreclosures of our choices, so we can even come to love them. Yes, we could keep the fantasy of possibilities alive, keep waiting for a clear sign that it's the right decision, or optimising our options, or we could simply find our spot on the couch and settle in.

Would you tell me, please, which way I ought to go from here? (I'm exhausted)

Sometimes the difficulty in decision making isn't so much feeling stifled by possibilities, but being overwhelmed by them.

While on paper more choice suggests a greater chance of finding the perfect fit, in reality it can lead to decision fatigue: that is, we become so tired of making decisions that our ability to make decisions worsens. This can have a ripple effect in our days and lives—when we are experiencing decision fatigue, we can wind up sweating the small stuff. As McGinnis said, 'When you are spending too much time worrying over what you're having for lunch, you are robbing yourself of the energy to focus on the things that matter.'

Exhausted sometimes by even the smallest choice, we can long for somebody to tell us what to do. I'm reminded of the scene from the television series *Fleabag*, created by Phoebe Waller-Bridge. In a confessional, the protagonist, Fleabag, tells The Priest that she knows exactly what she wants right now: 'I want someone to tell me what to wear every morning. I want someone to tell me what to eat, what to like, what to hate, what to rage about, what to listen to, what band to like, what to buy tickets for, what to joke about, what not to joke about. I want someone to tell me what to believe in, who to vote for, and who to love, and how to tell them. I just think I want someone to tell me how to live my life, Father, because so far I think I've been getting it wrong.'

When we're worried we're getting it all wrong, it can be a relief not to have to make decisions, to have someone to tell us what to do. Perhaps that's what pulls us to inspect the lives of successful people—we want to know what to do, when to do it and how to do it; they can limit our need to make decisions by giving us the answer that worked for them. At other times, of course, decisions are imposed upon us—by an illness, a demanding workload, a lockdown, a responsibility to a child or a loved one, financial circumstances, our mental health. For some, such experiences can bring a complicated feeling of relief along with the potential grief.

But perhaps there is a way to reduce decision fatigue without having to rely on imposed decisions or look to somebody else for the answer—after all, it is about finding what works for us.

I DIDN'T DO THE THING TODAY

In my conversations, I've encountered some novel approaches to dealing with the overwhelm of decisions. The artist and horticulturalist Annie Raser-Rowland, for example, reduces the number of decisions she makes in a day by being frugal. She doesn't buy new furniture or enter homeware stores, which typically are filled with things she doesn't need. This means that riffling through possibilities is minimised, and she avoids what she calls 'the fug of indecision'. Being frugal extends beyond spending habits, applying also to her attention: she feels no indecision over what to post on social media, for instance, because she doesn't use it.

Imposing our own limits can help reduce decision fatigue. We can spend less time sweating the small stuff and have more mental space for the big stuff. Having our own set of predetermined decisions—living frugally, perhaps, or creating a uniform for work—can help reduce the number of trivial decisions we have to make in our days. In turn, we have greater capacity to consider the important choices, whatever we deem them to be, or meet the urgent and unexpected decisions sprung upon us.

But even with the handy hints, at times I've still longed for someone to tell me what to do. Indeed, for a long while I would turn to friends, family, even practical strangers to help make a decision for me, only to find myself with a surplus of conflicting options.

As tempting as it may be to turn to other people for answers, only we can make our decisions. As the writer Ashley C. Ford told me, we can get into a bad habit of outsourcing our decisions to people who love us but don't have to live with the consequences. As an antidote, Ford recalled some advice she received from her mum: 'You are the only person who has to wake up and live in your skin.

I can't tell you what to do with your life. I can't tell you how it's going to feel because I don't have to wake up and be you.'

We might also get caught up worrying about what people might think of our decisions, so we turn to them for input to pre-emptively people-please. We might think that by asking for advice, we will be able to somehow please everyone, but in truth there's no such thing as a decision that makes everybody happy. In order to become more comfortable with our decisions, we can try experimenting for a day, a week or a month with making choices without asking for anyone's input or advice first.

Even though we might know intellectually that we can't please everybody and no one can make decisions for us, there will still be times we want to mull things over with someone we trust. This is quite different from decision by committee—it's seeking counsel. Sometimes, we don't even need to necessarily know someone whose counsel to seek. I often think of how the journalist Jamila Rizvi told me she has created a personal board of directors in her mind. She adopted the popular technique after hearing about its usefulness in dealing with criticism, but I think it can be applied to making decisions for ourselves, too. To circumvent worrying about what every stranger on the internet might think, we can create a list of ten people whose opinions matter most to us—it might include a dear friend, a former colleague, a sibling, a living idol, someone noteworthy from history, or even loved ones who may not be with us. As a prompt, I'll often read the poem 'My Dead Friends' by Marie Howe when I need a reminder to worry less and live more, or a way to find the answers I'm looking for. Perhaps not surprisingly, I've often found the best answers come from within me.

We can check in with our specially chosen few when making a choice, but remember to make sure to appoint yourself as chair—after all, this imaginary board is really a way to bring to the fore the opinion that matters most: yours.

Decision making is best as a process we craft for ourselves. We can tailor and adapt it, depending on whether we feel stifled or exhausted, whether we're facing something small or significant. We can ask for directions, but as the Cheshire Cat told Alice in Lewis Carroll's classic novel *Alice's Adventures in Wonderland*, it doesn't matter which way you go if you simply want to get somewhere: 'Oh, you're sure to do that, if only you walk long enough.'

A collection of choices for making choices

- For when you don't know what you want, try to focus on what you want to be—light-hearted, spontaneous, curious, brave.

- For when you're second-guessing whether something will make you happy, ask if it will expand or diminish your life.

- For when you're caught between two good options, imagine what your future day will look like. If you don't like the sight of a desk, then don't take the office job.

- For when you are fearful, make the choice that will put you more into the world and connect you with the people you cherish.

- For when neither choice is appealing, choose the problem you want to have—or, as Mae West put it, 'When choosing between two evils, I always like to try the one I've never tried before.'

- For trivial decisions, don't underestimate the simplicity of flipping a coin. Decision making is like building a muscle, and if we learn to do it well for the small things, we will do it better with the big things, too.

- For when you're unsure where a choice will take you, or if it's worth it, or will take too long, try to focus instead on what you might learn. The one thing we might never regret is learning something.

- For when you don't know where to start, focus on the step in front of you. Do the next necessary thing instead of tripping over yourself as you try to look 100 steps ahead.

- For when you're anxious and worried, try to recall your past successes and where you've encountered good things before.

- For when you're obsessing over the optimal decision for the future, shift your focus to what is satisfactory right now.

- For when you're worried about disappointing someone else, consider which regret you are willing to accept.

- For when you're choosing between camembert and brie, always choose brie. That is, choose the richer life experience.

- For when you're overthinking, step into your body and hold each choice, and notice which one takes the weight off your shoulders.

- For when you get the choice between diving more into life or sitting back, make sure you dive.

- For when you are weary and tired from the day, ask what someone who doesn't have the same opportunity as you might do. Remember you are alive—you've got options.

There is no such thing as the right decision

While we can do our best to reduce decision fatigue in our days, if we want to deal with the standstill of indecision once and for all, we would do well to recognise that we have far less control over the outcome of our decisions than we might think.

Some decisions can alter the course of our life in ways we can never predict. I'm reminded of a line from the film *Synecdoche, New York*: 'There are a million little strings attached to every choice you make; you can destroy your life every time you choose. But maybe you won't know for twenty years.'

What happens after we make a decision is contingent on countless variables: what other people do, what is going on in the world, the preceding and proceeding choices. Even when we look back and try to connect the dots, we see only faint outlines. We cannot trace the exact decision that led to our current circumstances, because we are perpetually playing them out—alongside the decision before that, and the one before that. In this ongoing course of both small and significant choices, it can be impossible to determine which have shaped who we are today.

So why do we obsess over whether we are making the right decision when there's no way to determine whether or not we have? We'll never meet the life we didn't choose. We'll never know if that life was better or worse. Even what we might think of as a wrong decision—say, enrolling in one university elective instead of another that was more compatible with our current career— might lead us to meet the person who is now our dearest friend. So perhaps we should focus on what we have done and can do, rather than on what we might have done.

And irrespective of whether we choose the 'right' or 'wrong' path, we might be very good at convincing ourselves retroactively that we chose correctly. A phenomenon known as 'choice-supportive bias' suggests that we have a tendency to ascribe positive attributes to the option we chose, and to demote whatever option we had to forgo—as Edith Piaf sang, *non, je ne regrette rien*.

Perhaps the best advice for facing indecision is to recognise that we can make a choice and it doesn't have to be the right one—because there is no such thing. Either it's impossible to determine how we got it right, or we will convince ourselves we were right in time.

Maybe we could save ourselves from the turmoil of indecision if we stop trying to find the 'right' choice and just go with what feels good right now in our hearts. That might sound trite, but if a pro and con list is, at best, projection, who is to say the heart can't be a better guide? I'm reminded of the words of writer Maya Angelou: 'I've learned that whenever I decide something with an open heart, I usually make the right decision.'

Employing our heart as a compass at least means that our decisions come from a deep sense of who we are and what we want—in as much as we can determine that, of course. To me, this is the essence of values-based decision making. Many years ago, I followed a simple exercise where I chose twenty words that resonated with me from a list of 100 values. The next step was to narrow the list down just to five. Over the course of a few days, I arrived at *integrity, curiosity, thoughtfulness, enjoyment* and *independence*. We can determine our own values in any number of ways, of course; perhaps we already know them intuitively.

If we know our own values, we have a way to engage our heart in the process of decision making. When we encounter an opportunity that might look great on paper but doesn't feel right, we have criteria against which we can check it. We often know we're making a decision with our heart when it feels like a weight has been taken off our shoulders when we consider a certain choice, or like we've swallowed a bundle of twinkle lights whole and can't stop beaming. Maybe getting to this point means we have gone around the indecision spiral a few times, but when we finally land on a choice, it feels like it fits.

Of course, a deep sense of who we are takes a long time to cultivate—and perhaps is ever-changing and therefore ever-elusive. Knowing this, we can keep an open heart instead of overthinking it: we can face just one 'what if' at time and make the best decision we can. Better yet, if we have the luxury of choice, we can choose the thing we really want.

We don't know who we will become tomorrow because we don't know where today's decisions will lead us. Nevertheless, each decision we make can refresh our days with change. That's part of the joy of living—to pave the path as we walk, and encounter the person who we will become as we go. So don't doubt your decisions, and don't worry about getting them right every time— because even the wrong ones can turn out to be right.

8

The Deflation of Comparison

No need to hurry. No need to sparkle.
No need to be anybody but oneself.

Virginia Woolf, *A Room of One's Own*

What other people *appear* to be doing or how well they appear to be doing it can easily make us feel that we're not doing enough or doing it well enough. We make snap judgements based on a sliver of someone's life: we deduce that they're having a better day, with a checked-off to-do list and a sunnier outlook, leaving us in despair at the messiness of our own life. Judging our lives against the surface of everyone else's is deflating, as we always wind up falling short.

Comparison can be a thief of joy, but it's a very human tendency. The social psychologist Leon Festinger used social comparison theory to describe our fundamental drive to self-evaluate and regulate our opinions, abilities and even emotions in comparison to those around us. This helps us to create an inner benchmark, and provides us with a sense of clarity as we define who we are and what works for us.

Yet for many, this function of comparison feels somewhat dampened by our modern lives. Surrounded as we are by opportunities to compare ourselves with others, we face a surplus of opinions and approaches that we must sort through. We're privy to much more than the goings-on of our inner circle: through our screens, we can have a front-row seat to the burgeoning careers, declarations of love, and fancy-free getaways of countless strangers.

We might find ourselves fixated on the perceived gap between our not-good-enough life and someone else's perfect one, not realising that we lack accurate reference points. We are making assumptions about someone else's life based on the vague outlines we see through our screens and own subjective looking glasses. What we're perceiving is just an approximation of someone else's reality—and it's highly likely they, too, have days when they didn't do the thing.

Intellectually, I realise I'm comparing my behind-the-scenes with someone's else highlights reel, but that knowledge doesn't necessarily temper my reaction. Instead, it's often the first trigger to prompt my sleuthing routine. In bouts of comparison, I've made a habit of combing through someone's Wikipedia page to measure myself against their timeline and trajectory. I'll become obsessed with gathering reference points to determine their age at various career milestones we share. If I haven't yet surpassed that age, I feel a momentary elation. If I have, it confirms I've fallen behind.

Feeling behind might inspire some people to play catch-up, but I'll often find myself halted. *It's too late*, I tell myself. *It's pointless to try—they are already so far ahead.* With a feeling of resignation, down a spiral I tumble, spinning until I'm too dizzy to make a start on something or appreciate the things I do have.

This deflating spiral of comparison can be a destructive indulgence. I can derail entire days in my preoccupation with somebody else's 'better' life, rather than focusing on living my own. This is where I find the comparison spiral can be a convenient distraction—it's easier to scatter our energy across what we covet in someone else's life than it is to acknowledge what we really want to do with our days, and what might bring us joy in our own lives.

But perhaps there is a way to wield our comparison constructively: as a guide that can enrich our days, rather than make them feel empty.

Curiosity as the cure for comparison

Comparison is not viewed in a particularly flattering light. While some of us may have more of a proclivity to comparison, it's something all of us learn to hide from view as it's seen as an 'ugly' emotion. This can make us feel alone in our tendency to compare, adding a layer of shame to the experience that only sends us deeper into our spiral. Perhaps, instead of distancing ourselves from comparison, we might benefit by getting closer to it.

Our encounters with the emotions that tend to niggle at us the most can be our greatest guide. In my conversation with psychotherapist Hilary Jacobs Hendel, I learned about using 'the change triangle' as a tool to identify our core emotions and use them as pointers for action. We can learn a lot from emotions, yet many of us have developed clever ways to inhibit them—either through shame, guilt or anxiety—or defend against them through behaviours ranging from procrastination to a deflecting sense of humour. Inhibitory emotions and our defences are the mind's way of protecting us from emotional pain and being overwhelmed by feelings, but they often keep us stuck in the spiral.

While it might sound counterintuitive, the best thing to do with our feelings and emotions is to allow them to flow. Working the change triangle is about trying to identify the core emotion beneath our defences or inhibitory emotions, to feel it, and then to approach it with curiosity, creativity or compassion. When we think about it this way, extracting ourselves from the comparison spiral becomes an exercise in curiosity—getting closer to the emotion so we can better understand it, feel it and use it as a guide.

When we get closer to envy, for example—the emotion that often underlies our urge to compare ourselves with others—we begin to notice that it can be as multifaceted as we are. The Dutch social psychologist Niels van de Ven pointed to two types of envy: malicious and benign. Both involve comparing ourselves to people we perceive as doing better in a particular area of life, or who have a particular quality, achievement or possession we lack. Where malicious envy wishes someone didn't have something we covet or wants to bring them down, benign envy focuses on the object of our desire and how we might get it too. In this way, benign envy is not only motivating, but can act as a map to what we want.

Over time, I've come to see that comparison has two different sides as well: empty and enriching. Both can catapult us into the deflating comparison spiral, but being able to distinguish between the types might help us find a way out.

Empty comparison often stems from inheriting or copying and pasting our life goals from other people. We might try to arrange our lives based on someone else's milestones or timeline, hoping to arrive at the same place they have. It's human nature to want to emulate someone we admire, but we have to make sure we don't lose sight of our own unique goals, talents and desires.

Enriching comparison, on the other hand, is defined by its ability to reveal to us what we really want, and to help us find our own way. Instead of trying to work out the precise step-by-step construction of someone's trajectory and layering it on top of our own, we can inspect individual components to see how they fit with our own blueprint. We can use comparison to notice and chart what it is we really want—and how we can get there in our own way.

How can we know the difference? Where empty comparison leaves us fixating on whether we are ahead or behind, enriching comparison propels us into action. Where empty comparison can lead us astray, enriching comparison leads us to what we want. Where empty comparison attaches itself to recognition, possessions and validation, enriching comparison brings us closer to what we enjoy doing for its own sake. Where empty comparison tells us that someone else's success means there's less available for us, enriching comparison reminds us that what other people do can't diminish what we do.

Even with these guidelines in mind, it will not always be clear whether our comparison is enriching or empty, so we have to get closer and explore what we are feeling. I've found that being curious about the people we are comparing ourselves with to be one of the greatest salves to comparison.

Often, when we listen, our comparison brings questions: *When did everyone figure out their lives? When did they learn how to be good at their jobs, their craft, their relationship, their friendships, their passions, their cares—and how do they balance it all with ease?* If we apply curiosity and listen attentively to the lives of others instead of our own projections, we might find comforting answers.

This was certainly the case for me. Thinking about it now, these very questions—and the comparisons behind them—were the main impetus behind my decision to interview creative people about their days. I wanted to know how they figured out their lives so I could figure out my life too. And I believe that very endeavour began to soften my comparison urge. The conversations dismantled the pedestal I was placing people on, and helped me see something far more interesting: a person who, just like me, was still figuring it out.

People generously shared with me their experiences of feeling behind, of procrastination, of rejection, of distraction, of stagnation, of worry, of yearning, of dissatisfaction. I was able to hear first-hand how success takes years, you have to be patient, you can change your mind, you can let go. We just don't get all that when we read a Wikipedia page or scroll an Instagram feed.

We can easily be duped by our own projections about how easy it must be for everyone else, and come to the conclusion that there must be something wrong with us for finding it hard. But what we don't see can be the advantages people may have had through wealth, education or opportunity. While privilege (often unseen) can greatly aid success, it's difficult for everyone to figure out how to navigate their own life. When we get up close to others, ask questions or pay attention, we not only recognise the different starting points people have had, but we also see the shared doubts. We begin to feel more at ease about our way of doing things, because we discover there is more than one way of doing things.

So when you're comparing yourself to someone else, try to get up close to that person's life; otherwise you're comparing yourself to a hologram. When we reach out to a friend to congratulate them on an envy-inducing award or new job, our faulty projections start to fade when they tell us how hard they worked for it. We find out that their partner looked after the kids every morning for three months so they could wake pre-dawn to complete a qualification, or that they've been rejected six times before finally achieving this success.

Another benefit to getting up close to someone else's life is that we begin to ask with curiosity if we really do want that life. Instead of being hung up on the things we don't have or can't have, we can consider what it is that we truly want. This question is particularly helpful for determining if our comparison is empty. When we encounter someone we admire or who has done something impressive, our knee-jerk reaction can be to strive to emulate them. But in such haste we might be ignoring the fact that their path is completely incompatible with our own wants, aims or temperament. We can easily miss what *we* really want when we keep getting lost in other people's lives. We berate ourselves for not doing the thing today, forgetting that it's actually someone else's thing.

Curiosity can also help diminish empty comparison by revealing to us that something isn't for us. There's only one timeline or trajectory that matters—the one with the plateaus, dips, falls, ascents and redirections: the one that's yours.

Enriching comparison, by contrast, lights us up to what we want—but it's generally a slow burn, not a flash in the pan. It can guide us to the thing we didn't know we longed for, or didn't think we were worthy of. Instead of telling us it's too late or we have fallen behind, enriching comparison surprises us by whispering, 'Maybe we can do that too.'

Following our secret joy

Comparison doesn't have to be the thief of joy—it can prompt us to be curious, alert us to our secret joy, and inspire us to bring more of what we want into our lives.

Enriching comparisons ask us to consider what we really want, and to go deeper than what we see on the surface. This is what I call our secret joy—and I give it that name because often we keep it secret from ourselves.

We find our secret joy a few layers beneath the comparisons we make. A few years ago, I started to keep a comparison diary, taking note of who I was comparing myself with and then looking for patterns. My diary revealed a collection of writers, poets, activists, illustrators, community builders and podcasters. At first glance, my comparison didn't seem to reveal anything to me that I didn't already know—I knew I wanted to start a podcast, to write, to engage in what mattered to me. But reading between the things I wanted to *do*, I saw what I wanted to *be*: patient, dedicated, curious.

Our secret joy doesn't live in a list of names, impressive achievements or things to add to the to-do list—it's found in what that list represents to us.

We will know it's our secret joy when it's yearning for a quality, not a possession or milestone. It helps us see that if we want something, we have to create it for ourselves. Maybe it's directing us to dedicate ourselves to a new skill. Maybe it's telling us to work at it for a few more years and be patient. Maybe it's hinting that we should connect with our friends more and build fun into our days. Maybe it's setting boundaries so we have space.

We can also cast a wide net when we are using comparison to find our secret joy. Comparison can also time-travel, with a little imagination. When we compare, it's usually in reference to the society we live in or the social circles we move in, which makes it easy for us to feel stuck and confined. I rather liked Annie Raser-Rowland's liberating idea of comparing ourselves to anyone in history, in order to remember that we can do things differently. As she told me, 'There are so many human lifestyles throughout time and a lot of wiggle room in who you compare yourself to— you just have to keep reminding yourself that it doesn't just have to be your best friends.'

Our secret joy is life-giving, rather than life-depleting. Instead of siphoning off our energy to what's happening outside ourselves, we can start to move towards the very things we yearn for. I remember speaking with the artist, designer and author Beci Orpin about how comparison can distract us from doing the things we really want to do. Early in her career, she told me, she put a lot of energy into comparing herself to her peers. 'Even though

I was having my own successes,' she said, 'in my eyes it paled in comparison to what they were experiencing at a similar stage of their careers.'

Then Beci had the realisation that she could direct that same energy into her own wants, her own career. This created the space for her to do the thing and thereby experience more success in her own work. 'Once I stopped comparing myself and worrying about what other people were doing, that energy was redirected,' she said. 'I started to worry about what I was doing and worked hard towards that.'

When we follow our secret joy, the urge to compare begins to dissipate. We begin to understand what we really want, and in pursuing that joy, we find that what everybody else is doing doesn't seem to matter as much. When we place the emphasis back on ourselves by attending to what we want to do, we also find ourselves turning our heads less and focusing more on what is in front of us. It becomes easier to continue to do what we really want to do because we aren't as derailed by what someone else appears to be doing.

It's important to note that following your secret joy isn't always joyful—doing the work in front of us can be quite hard. But just because something is hard doesn't mean it's not worth doing. I think that's what we begin to internalise when we follow our secret joy—that just because we haven't arrived yet, that doesn't mean it's not a worthy path to pursue. We have to become comfortable with starting wherever we find ourselves, not where we perceive someone else to be.

My tendency to compare hasn't gone away; perhaps the difference is that I no longer feel comparison needs to be something

I have to change about myself. Rather, I now see a bout of comparison as something I can be curious about and take notice of so that it can become the enriching variety. This perspective may not entirely prevent us from falling into the comparison spiral, but it can help bring us out—like an elastic rope attached to a bungee jumper, our secret joy can pull us back up before we make a thud. Instead of looking for evidence about whether I'm ahead of or behind someone else, I can look for things I may wish to try—and find joy in my own process instead of turning my head at someone else.

More and more, the direction I find myself glancing in isn't upwards or downwards, but inwards. We tend to spiral in what's called 'upward social comparison', comparing ourselves to those who appear to be further ahead. But we can also turn our attention back to where we were a few years ago, and cultivate appreciation for where we may be in our own lives. Instead of comparing timelines and tracking accomplishments, assessing whether we're ahead or behind, we can create our own scorecard. Who were we yesterday, last year, a decade ago?

Perhaps by looking inward instead of at everybody else, we can finally find the value in the messy parts, the rejections, the moments we thought were behind. These are the experiences that are pivotal in making us who we are today: someone incomparable.

9

The Great Disappointment
of Expectation

*The greatest obstacle to living is expectancy, which hangs
upon tomorrow and loses today . . . The whole future
lies in uncertainty: live immediately.*

Lucius Annaeus Seneca, *On the Shortness of Life*

Before the day has begun, there can be an exceedingly high bar
to reach: to get up at a certain time, to attend to a long to-do list, to
somehow be everywhere at once. And when—even with the hours
swaddled by our plans—the day unfolds differently, we encounter
a familiar sense of guilt and self-blame. But perhaps the reason we
didn't do the thing today isn't because of our shortcomings, but
simply that our expectations of the day were too great.

Such expectations often come hand-in-hand with excessive
standards of constant improvement, unrelenting upward traject-
ories, doing more and more. When we fall short, instead of adjusting

our expectations, we create more for tomorrow: *I should wake up earlier. I should be more productive. I should be more organised. I should exercise more. I should have finished this project by now. I should get my life together.*

Sure, some of these things might bring vitality into our days, but the worrisome word here is *should*. When we grasp too tightly onto how something *should* be, we can be knocked over by the slightest change—even if it's inconsequential, or even if it's positive. It's not what we expected, *what we deserved.*

Despite what we tell ourselves, a should isn't going to solve our quandaries—it simply crams more expectation between the lines of our to-do lists that we can't keep up with. The should bucket all too quickly overflows, drenching us in our own perceived disappointments.

We aren't solely responsible for stamping our days and lives with expectations—we are surrounded by them. There are those we place on ourselves, societal expectations, cultural expectations, the expectations others have for us (or don't), and the expectations we imagine they have.

Judging our lives based on whether we have fulfilled an expectation can create a gap between our present-day reality and what we think our lives should be. We compare who we are today with who we wish to become, and find ourselves once more in the deflating gap of comparison. Expectations, it would seem, lead to misery. This is affirmed when we look up famous words on expectations and find variations on a theme: expectations lead to disappointment.

Of course, expectations aren't all bad—it can be a sign of self-belief to expect a lot of ourselves, to strive for something important to us, to know what we deserve. Creating an expectation—making a plan—can both buoy us and propel us forward. After all, isn't hope a form of expectation? It was Jane Austen, in *Sense and Sensibility*, who wrote that 'to wish was to hope, and to hope was to expect'.

Expectations can remind us what we might change in our days, or what we want in life, becoming the springboard we need to make a hopeful start. If we didn't expect more of ourselves, we might not try to quit a bad habit, apply for a new job or try our hand at something new—or perhaps even set an alarm to get to work on time. There can be a soft bigotry to placing low expectations on others, too. When other people or society expect more of us, that can imbue us with confidence. The inherent hope of expectations can instil confidence in the world, too—we can expect more of leaders, of organisations, of our collective humanity.

But sometimes our expectations of ourselves or of others can disappoint us, and other times they can cloud our view. Hope itself may be a veil—it can prevent us from acknowledging something we fear or consider unjust, and consequently from doing the work to confront it. Concealing our fears with hope might make things more palatable, but if we avoid inspecting fear and injustice—in ourselves or the world around us—it can lead to complacency. It's only in finally seeing what we are afraid of that we can find ways to address it.

Perhaps there is a place for pessimism when it comes to our personal expectations. When we acknowledge that a situation will not always be hopeful, or that some expectations are impossible to meet, we can put ourselves in a better position to look for solutions. We can assess our hope—whether it's having a certain career, finding love, starting a family, finding creative success—and ask the question we have been avoiding: can I still find something in my days, some vitality, without this? What if things never change? Can I still find something to enjoy about my life?

Of course, pessimism can present its own problems—we can turn from having hope to feeling hopeless. It might be helpful to think back to the idea of being a time realist and a time optimist, and apply that theory to our expectations. Being an expectation optimist may see us overcrowd our days in the naive hope we can achieve it all. Yet if we can be an expectation realist—and understand we might not get everything done in a day, for example—we might be more realistic about the expectations we place on ourselves.

Perhaps what's most corrosive to our ability to feel good about the day is when we keep trying to do so much in a day that we only disappoint ourselves. Expectations are like tiny promises in our days that can knock us over. If we are more realistic about our expectations, we are more likely to keep the promises we make to ourselves and feel good about the things we did do.

And we may be more adaptable to our human fallibility, too. When I interviewed the advice columnist and author Heather Havrilesky, she told me that some days she plans to create, and some days she ends up eating muffins. It's a relatable admission— each of us has no doubt reached for our snack of choice instead of keeping a promise to ourselves. But it's also an acknowledgement that the day can unfold differently from what we'd planned— often we don't take into account the unexpected but inevitable meetings that run overtime, transit delays, impromptu phone calls or personal responsibilities. We also fail to consider how long the minutiae of our day takes—cleaning, chores, grocery shopping, picking up the kids, getting caught in traffic, going to an appointment. But sometimes things go off track for no apparent reason at all—it's just a muffin kind of day. Perhaps, instead of berating ourselves for those days, we can go with them. Instead of trying to clear away the crumbs, we can enjoy the day for what it is.

Instead of pinning our great hopes onto tomorrow, we can be okay with holding our disappointments in our days: we can find ways to live with them, and maybe we'll find something great within them too. We can ask what we want from this day, rather than be directed by what we expect the day should be.

Holding expectations lightly

We don't need to abandon all expectations or the hope that comes with them, but rather learn how we can let go of our attachment to particular outcomes. By definition, an expectation is a strong belief that something will happen or will be the case. There's an element of certainty to an expectation. For better or worse, it's a feeling that there is a guarantee—it's a bid for control, when of course we can't control the future. Just like feelings, expectations shift and move. Yet we are disappointed when something moves beyond our grasp. So we hold on tightly, make plans or add more shoulds—only for them to shatter. As Brandon Sanderson wrote in *The Way of Kings*, 'Expectations were like fine pottery. The harder you held them, the more likely they were to crack.'

We think we're controlling our lives by setting up expectations, but we can be narrowing them. I have long tried to pin down my expectations by turning them into plans. I'd make list upon list of everything I want to do in the next decade, year, month and week, and make a daily event out of trying to mould my life. I recently found one list that I drafted when I was 27. It was a list of 100 things I wanted to do before I turned 30: run ten kilometres, publish a book, take singing lessons, learn a language, ferment foods, live in New York City, live in the Italian countryside, deliver a TED Talk, live alone in an apartment I own, have an amorous love affair. I distributed each of these to-do items across five six-month blocks, convinced my life plan was taking shape in a spreadsheet. I didn't realise it was actually in the sky.

Of course, planning can give shape to the day. As I overheard a teenager say at the bus stop, 'If I don't have anything planned I just stay at home and then feel disgusting about myself.' Some level of planning is necessary so we don't feel like shapeless blobs, as well as to manage conflicting priorities, appease demanding schedules and ensure we don't delay others. But there is a difference between planning that is preparation and planning that is driven by anxiety, restlessness or fear of uncertainty.

Whether it's how our careers will pan out, the shifting outline of a pandemic or the outcome of an election, uncertainty can make our days feel unsteady. A plan, a list, an expectation for how things will go is a way of stepping outside our life in order to control it—if I am the creator of a plan of 100 things I want to do, then maybe I can influence how my future will unfold. I have noticed in myself and others that in writing a plan, I'm searching for more than order—I'm trying to pinpoint where I can exercise control and eliminate my fear of the unknown. I'm creating a vision for my future self where the tumbles of today will no longer get in the way.

But our plans don't shield us from such unknowns—our days unfold in unexpected ways, list or no list. A plan is an attempt to write a future so it feels more certain, more ideal, more productive, more pleasant, but it's often in vain. As Arnold Bennett wrote in *How to Live on 24 Hours a Day*, 'If you imagine that you will be able to achieve your ideal by ingeniously planning out a timetable with a pen on a piece of paper, you had better give up hope at once.'

We cannot rid our futures of uncertainty, but we can loosen our grip on our desire for certainty. We can change our great expectations of our future self, and relieve some of the pressure. When I find myself grasping my plans too tightly, I try to soften them into intentions rather than expectations. An intention is lighter—it's an aim, rather than an assumption. It's a gentle guide, where an expectation is a prescriptive outcome. Where expectations fixate on how a goal should look—say, to cook the perfect meal—intentions emphasise the experience around the goal—say, to enjoy the meal with the people you love.

A few years ago, I made this shift from expectations to intentions in how I framed my new year's resolutions. Instead of writing down an overcrowded list of unrealistic goals that would inevitably lead to disappointment, as well as guilt, anxiety or shame, I now pick just one word as a gentle focus. In previous years, chosen words have included *joy, momentum, trust, merely*. There's no outcome or expectation; holding a word allows for the unexpected shift and invites us to become curious about how the year unfolds.

An intention can show us the way, but it doesn't predetermine the way. This reminds me of how the designer Ryder Carroll—the creator of the popular Bullet Journal method—described his approach to setting goals. He chooses to see them as lighthouses, since a ship never steers towards the lighthouse; it's used as a guide. As Ryder told me, 'Redefining our goals as guides rather than destinations takes the blinders off. It helps us shed our expectations, and allows us to take in the whole picture.' Intentions can be lighthouses that illuminate the safe passages to follow, but also that allow us to adjust course as necessary. Sometimes we'll find ourselves at a destination we did not expect, and that's part of the fun.

Intentions are less stifling than expectations or rigid plans. Expecting so much of ourselves can curtail our ability to do something—either by exacerbating our feelings of being already behind or by setting us up to fail. When we don't do something right the first time, or when we fall short of our expectations, we can take it as proof that we're incapable and never try again.

Perhaps, instead of giving up after our first try, we'd do better to ask whether the expectations we set are unrealistic to begin with. When I spoke with the writer Ashley C. Ford, she told me how setting unrealistic expectations for herself was essentially an excuse. 'It was a way for me to convince myself I'm not the kind of person who can do a certain thing, when the truth is, maybe you're not the kind of person who over a weekend can decide to give up sugar, start waking up at six o'clock, start meditating, start learning calligraphy, and all this other stuff. Maybe you are the person who could wake up a half-hour earlier tomorrow.'

You haven't failed—you've simply failed to meet an expectation that was perhaps discretionary or too great to begin with. To hold something lightly, it must be right-sized. Maybe, instead of expecting ourselves to overhaul our lives completely with an itemised spreadsheet, we should pick just one small thing? Instead of expecting ourselves to write a thousand words each morning, why not focus on just one paragraph? Instead of starting training for a marathon, why not jog around the block?

It's a quiet form of self-sabotage to attempt to do too much at the beginning—to try to hold something that's too heavy. But one of the greatest antidotes to the overwhelm of expectation is to start small. Expectations can be stifling because they ignore our tendency to make mistakes, to faff, to flail, to be interrupted and distracted. So maybe set the bar lower. Simplify. Be okay with it taking twice as long. Break your expectations into such small steps that you no longer trip over or are unable to move forward. Sometimes, when everything feels particularly uncertain, we don't need another plan—we simply need to be okay with the unknown and do the thing anyway. Doing the thing often comes before feeling good about the thing—but so often we wait until everything is right and good before we begin something. While planning can increase our motivation, or soothe us from the fear of uncertainty, it can go awry because we aren't very good at estimating how much is feasible. As an antidote, we can become near-term planners— planning what you're doing in the next hour is much more feasible than planning for the day, let alone for the next year or decade. As C.S. Lewis put it in *The Weight of Glory*, 'Happy work is best done by the man who takes his long-term plans somewhat lightly and works from moment to moment.' Perhaps that's what we can actually control—doing the thing in the moment we are in. We can also trip over our negative expectations—after all, an expectation can be one of dread just as much as of hope. We can see an opportunity and tell ourselves that we're not good enough. By rejecting ourselves before others reject us, we hold ourselves back from the things we want. Again, we can hold our expectations lightly as intentions—we can simply express our interest, put our hat in the ring, ask with curiosity. We can plan less and do more.

Whether we're daunted or hopeful, how things turn out is bound to be different from what we expect. Looking back at my list of 100 things makes me both chuckle and gasp at myself—who was this 27-year-old who thought she could publish a book, curate an exhibition, buy an apartment and acquire a language in less than three years—as well as learn to ferment, to juggle, to play piano and to sing, and split her time between New York City and Italy? She was hopeful and excited, yes, but also hard on herself when it came to the specific timelines, shapes and ways in which things should unfold.

Revisiting that list now, when I'm in my thirties, is interesting. Some things, I see, have worked themselves out. I don't own an apartment, but I live alone in a rental. I don't ferment vegetables, but I can play one song on the piano. Reflecting on this rather trivial exercise has helped me see that the wonder is in not quite knowing, not in the planning. As the poet Wendell Berry said in an interview with *Humanities* magazine, 'Unexpected wonders happen, not on schedule, or when you expect or want them to happen, but if you keep hanging around, they do happen.'

Perhaps, instead of a rigid life plan, we can hold wishes for our future selves. In July 2005, the renowned New York designer Debbie Millman took a summer intensive course taught by the veteran graphic designer Milton Glaser. He instructed the class to write an essay describing the life they could have had if they'd pursued everything they wanted, with the certainty that they would have had success in each endeavour. Dream big, he said, don't edit, and be careful what you wish for—there was a magical quality to this essay he had observed again and again in his students.

Millman was not immune to such magic, as she explained to me. 'I think it was twelve things that I was hoping for and I think eleven of them have come true. They were big, audacious things. It's spooky.' Now an educator, Millman has since modified the essay exercise and teaches it to her students at the School of Visual Arts in New York. She has observed that the more detail and care students take in their essays—from what their careers look like to the minutiae of their daily lives in ten years' time—the more success they ultimately have.

What I like about the ten-year plan, as opposed to my previous itemised and dated spreadsheet, is that it's not about looking for specific goals, but looking for a way of life and holding that wish lightly. After it is written, it is best kept tucked away in a drawer, away from view, leaving you open to the moment. Then one day you might stumble on it or return to it, and be surprised by the wishes that have been fulfilled. The exercise also encourages us to be delighted by the possibility of the future, rather than daunted by it. Instead of worrying, we might make the big wishes for the future, but fold them away gently in the back of our mind so we can go about making the most of what we have in this day—and allow unexpected wonders to happen on their own.

Perhaps that's what we can come to appreciate. When we hold a plan lightly, we can be more attuned to the possibilities that lie before us, rather than fixating on whether everything went to plan.

We might even find that the joy is in the cells of the spreadsheet we left blank, or what we have not yet done. I've long thought an incomplete to-do list reflected my own sense of incompletion. As the physicist Marie Curie wrote in a letter to her brother in 1894, 'One never notices what has been done; one can only see what remains to be done.' Things began to change for me when I stopped looking at my list as one enumerating my failures, but rather as one of possibilities.

There's a power in the word *yet*—perhaps we didn't yet do the thing, and yet we still can. For me, this idea is helpful. Rather than feeling overwhelmed by what's left to do, we can be guided by it—and perhaps even excited by all the things we still have time to explore. We can sit with the undone, while we also appreciate what we have done.

Taking an inventory of our shoulds

Rather than dismissing the days that didn't meet our expectations, perhaps it's the unrealistic shoulds and the onerous obligations that we need to strike.

Shoulds accumulate from many sources, but it's our self-imposed shoulds that may be the easiest to spot—for me, anyway, they are front and centre on my to-do lists. In *How Do We Know We're Doing It Right?*, the journalist Pandora Sykes wrote, 'When I moan about how busy I am, what I actually mean is that I have a lot that I should be doing.' Our lists of shoulds is of our own making—and so is our subsequent misery.

External expectations can be harder to trace. We may have internalised the notion that we should expect more from ourselves in

school, in our careers, in our personal lives, in our relationships—
and built our identities around such expectations. In the last three
generations, according to the psychoanalyst Esther Perel, much of
Westernised culture has shifted into an 'identity economy', bringing
with it more personal freedom but also struggles with uncertainty,
loneliness and self-doubt. We've turned to work as more than a
means to an end: it's where we expect our emotional, physical and
psychological needs to be met. As Perel put it, 'Work is no longer
just what you do, but who you are.'

When we conflate who we are with what we do, it's perhaps
no wonder we crowd numerous shoulds onto our to-do lists—it
helps us feel tethered to something. But if to tether is to restrict, do
we really want to restrict ourselves, to narrow who we are? When we
tie who we are to what we do, we can get stuck in an 'if only'
spiral—we might say we are a runner, for example, but then shame
ourselves when we don't manage to run every day. We make the
mistake of labelling ourselves as nouns, when we are really verbs—
we are not a runner, but rather a person who runs; we're not a
writer, but a person who writes. Our sense of self doesn't have to be
bundled up with whether we did the thing today—because we are
not the things we do.

Perhaps being okay with being untethered from what we
did or did not do is a better way to live with the ambiguities of
life. In leaving ourselves undefined, we have the space to become
anything—or at the very least to be flexible and adaptive to the
changes we'll encounter.

To untether ourselves from our shoulds, we may first need to
recognise them. Naturally, we can't simply drop everything we

don't want to do at any given moment. The lines between a should and a responsibility may become confused, but there's a distinct difference between the two. A should is an expectation placed on us by ourselves or by others; when inspected, it might seem flat, expired, empty or heavy. A responsibility, however, might not be something we wish to do—it might be uncomfortable, or boring, or difficult, but is essential, or something we can't avoid without letting others down. For a people-pleaser, it might be difficult to determine whether something is a responsibility or a should, because we don't want to disappoint people, so an additional question could be whether something is congruent with our values or the kind of person we want to be, not just what we feel like doing. Sometimes disappointing someone is the price we pay for acknowledging what is or is not our responsibility.

When I've got an inkling that I'm carrying too many shoulds in my days, I'll often write out my entire to-do list so I can see it on the page—every should, task, commitment, job, project, idea, correspondence and chore that I can think of. When I survey the list, more often than not I'll see a page filled with superfluous shoulds—expired ideas, unessential commitments, tasks that can wait. Instead of carrying something over to tomorrow's to-do list for the tenth time, I can ask: *What is essential? What can I cross off? What can I delegate or come back to later?*

After doing this exercise, I'll often see with clarity that there are things I've been carrying in my mental to-do list that are merely shoulds, but I've covered this truth up with clever excuses. I've told myself I'll do it when work has settled, when I get a better desk, or after I get back from a holiday. I keep saying I'll get to

I DIDN'T DO THE THING TODAY

it 'soon', when actually I don't really want to do it, because many opportunities for 'now' have passed. The thing no longer brings me alive, and I can let it go. Shedding our shoulds isn't always easy. We can re-create the sunk cost fallacy across our days. That is, we focus on how much time, energy, money or attention we may have already poured into something, rather than seeing the benefit in freeing ourselves—and our time, energy, money and attention— for something else. When we let go of one thing, we may feel a sense of loss and even grief—but there will also be new-found space for another thing. As the illustrator Oslo Davis reminded me in our conversation, it's okay to give up on ideas, projects or things when it's an option. Continuing to do something out of expectation, obligation or a prior investment of energy is far more onerous than moving on. 'It can be okay to abandon a project or admit something isn't working,' he said. 'You don't have to read to the end of a book—or finish a terrible gin and tonic—out of obligation. Obligation stifles creativity.'

There is an art to letting go—it requires us to try at something, and sometimes try again, but also to know when to cut our losses and move on to the next thing. It's an art especially when others are intertwined in our obligations. It can be difficult to let go of a should when we feel like we are disappointing people, or that someone else might not manage without us. Yet often our attempt to carry someone else's expectations or plans is simply our own way to grasp for control over the people or things around us. If we can become more comfortable letting go of what is not ours to carry, we create space not only for ourselves to honour our own wants, but also for others to do the same.

Letting go is an art, as well, because it confronts our sense of identity, making us question who we are if we don't do that thing anymore—if what we do is no longer who we are. For decades, the environmentalist John Francis defined himself both by his decision not to use motor vehicles out of respect for the earth and by his choice not to speak. But after taking a monumental silent trek, he realised he had become imprisoned by these identify-defining choices. 'It took me 100 miles to figure out that, in my heart, in me, I had become a prisoner,' he said in his TED Talk, titled 'Walk the Earth . . . My 17-Year Vow of Silence', 'and I needed to escape.'

We can make important, identifying commitments in our lives, but we often neglect checking in with ourselves about whether they still serve us. We become attached to our identities— as morning people, as diligent news readers, as partnered or single people, as multitaskers, as self-employed workers, as managing directors—without asking ourselves if our circumstances still require that routine, that paycheque or that type of love.

Francis was afraid to change because he was used to being the person who just walked. 'I was so used to that person that I didn't want to stop,' he said. 'I didn't know who I would be if I changed. But I know I needed to. I know I needed to change, because it would be the only way that I could be here today.' I need to remind myself of Francis's message often: sometimes we have to let go of what we want to be, in favour of what we are becoming.

For a long while, I thought I had to work really hard to fill the space left when I let go of something, but sometimes things are a lot easier for us and those around us when we simply let go and be okay with the gap between no longer and not yet.

We can still have self-determination and ideas about what or who we want to be, but it's important that our grip is loose enough that we can let go when that is our best option. Perhaps our life improves when we let go of how we think it should be, and simply give ourselves enough space to experience each day for what it is.

So the next time you go through your to-do list and scrape all those flat, expired, empty and heavy shoulds from your plate, try resisting the urge to fill the space they leave. Instead, simply be open to the surprise of the day. As John Francis said, 'Part of the mystery of walking is that the destination is inside us and we really don't know when we arrive until we arrive.'

You can't arrange life; it happens around you

Shoulds are peppered throughout our lives, not just on our to-do lists—we should go to college, we should get a certain job, we should climb the ladder to success, we should get married, we should buy a home, we should have children. A life can be laid out for us in shoulds—but do we want that life?

When we're drafting plans, often we're trying to answer the question of how. How will I succeed in my career? How will I find love? How will I ever shape the life I want? Asking how can be another way we attempt to control what's uncertain in our lives. And so we get caught in a loop of overthinking the how of life, instead of simply doing it. We won't know how until we begin, but still we sit on the sidelines, looking for answers. I'm reminded of a line in the film *Under the Tuscan Sun*, where the eccentric, ageing actress Katherine, played by Lindsay Duncan, tells the protagonist, Frances, 'Listen, when I was a little girl I used to spend hours looking for ladybugs. Finally, I'd just give up and fall asleep in the grass. When I woke up, they were crawling all over me.'

Instead of repeatedly asking how, we can focus on what we want and let the how take care of itself—because the how is always going to find its own way. This isn't to suggest that we can simply fall asleep in the grass and everything we want will come to us, but perhaps we can recognise that the work we think we should be doing—and the hours spent looking, planning, asking how—won't take us any closer either.

Determining what we want isn't necessarily straightforward. We might not know what we want, we might find it uncomfortable to want something or we might even feel ashamed of our wants. To want is to set your heart on something, and revealing what we want means sharing what's in your heart.

We won't know what our heart wants if we have borrowed our wants from other people, or subscribed to what we're told to want. Society is impatient when it comes to our figuring out what we want—from a young age we are asked what we want to be when we grow up, what we want to study, what we want in a partner, what we want our dream home to look like, what we want to own and possess, what we want our lives to amount to. What if we don't know the answers yet? What if our wants change over time? What if we don't feel worthy of the wanting?

It's confronting to want something different, because there's more unknown—the path has not yet been paved. We follow the well-trodden path as a means of ensuring a safe passage, or to avoid explaining ourselves to others, or so we don't feel like the odd one out. Yet such wants can feel empty or shallow. As the philosopher

Alan Watts put it in the speech 'What if Money Were No Object', they are 'all retch and no vomit'. When we prioritise these borrowed wants, we risk spending our lives never doing the things we want to do—or, as Watts said, 'You'll be doing things you don't like doing in order to go on living, that is to go on doing things you don't like doing, which is stupid. Better to have a short life full of what you like doing, than a long life spent in a miserable way.'

What we are really looking for is the deeper want—not something on the surface but something that is all-encompassing. It comes back to finding congruence with ourselves, a compatibility with our wants. A deeper, all-encompassing want doesn't feel borrowed, but like our very own. A deeper want brings a sense of aliveness—in the same way a secret joy does—and can often take us by surprise.

A great human contradiction, for many of us, is that we feel uneasy when faced with uncertainty and chaos, yet uninspired by predictability. Often, what we really want isn't something we could have expected or planned for—if everything went to plan, if everything was completely predictable, if everything was certain, our days would be lacklustre. Our lives would be devoid of meaning because there would be nothing to learn, nothing to manoeuvre, nothing to solve.

We don't really want to control everything, or for our plans to unfurl in perfect order—we want the possibilities of life to be a surprise. We want something left to discover. We don't want the spoiler. We don't want a plan to get in the way of a good opportunity. Of course, not all surprises in life are welcome—they can be the very thing that derails our plans: such as an accident, an upset, the unexpected loss of a beloved family pet. But whether positive or negative, what a surprise often gives us is more than an expectation or plan ever can—it plants us in the day, and can be the catalyst for paying attention, for curiosity, for seeing the world differently, for breaking the monotony, for a whole new life.

Much like the stifling pursuit of trying to make the right decisions, our plans and expectations overlook that the most enriching opportunities in life aren't something we can plan for—most things in life are a surprise. Whether it's the people we come to love, friendships, career paths or new interests, most of the things that give our lives meaning we never saw coming.

I remember attending a talk with the food writer and celebrity chef Nigella Lawson, where she said her career has been a surprise. Working as a journalist, it never occurred to her that food would play any part in her career until her husband said she should write a book and call it *How to Eat*. 'I thought this was a nonsensical idea,' she said, 'but I did write it, and I wrote it because cooking had been dominated by professionals . . . I think a lot of young people think you can plan everything—you can't plan anything. Well you can plan if you want to, but it's pretty pointless.'

For the most part, this has been a common theme among the people I've interviewed—their careers have come as a surprise to them. Sometimes it's been a result of doing things even if they don't know why or have a particular outcome in mind, and it makes sense later on. Others may have had a strong idea of what they wanted, but there wasn't a clear recipe for success—they just did the best they could with the ingredients they were given.

When we know what our tomorrows will bring, we can feel existential malaise. Of course, for some people or in some circumstances, we don't want surprises—we want stability. But maybe all of us can see that the best things in our lives—the people we know, the opportunities we couldn't have dreamed of—are usually a surprise.

When each of us looks back on our days, we often find it to be true that the things that didn't go to plan—the things that surprised us—were more crucial to the making of us than the things that did. And there's always more to surprise us—we are yet to meet new people we will love and who will love us, we are yet to discover new things we will enjoy, we are yet to learn so many things about the world and ourselves. It might sound counterintuitive, but I believe we can create more space in our days for such formative surprises—we can leave room in our schedules, reach out to friends for a spontaneous walk, follow our whims.

When I was speaking with Heather Havrilesky, she'd just published her book, *What If This Were Enough?*, and was navigating the rut that often follows a big project or the achievement of a life goal. 'I'm experimenting with just following my whims wherever they lead as a means of being kind to myself and being free and feeling inspired,' she told me. 'I feel like it's somehow paying off. I have a lightness around the process that I didn't have before.'

There are so many things we are implicitly and explicitly told to be—smart, wise, fit, beautiful, successful, wealthy (the very prescriptions that often lead us into a rut). An instruction to be whimsical feels, to me, not only more accessible but more conducive to fostering the very creativity we need to discover our deeper wants.

Being whimsical invites playfulness and curiosity, and embraces uncertainty because it is directionless. Whimsy helps us veer off the well-trodden path and break free from our self-perpetuating cycles. Whimsy requires us to inspect what's around us and see where something leads. It breaks down the idea that productivity is the only measure of our worthiness, or even that there must be a measurable outcome for our efforts. Our whims take us to new places—and often require that we go out on a limb and step into something that is not yet defined, something uncertain—whether that means facing the blank page or investing our time into a new project. Perhaps the greatest advice on this came from David Bowie, featured in the documentary *David Bowie: The Last Five Years*: 'Always go a little further into the water than you feel you're capable of being in. Go a little bit out of your depth and when you don't feel that your feet are quite touching the bottom, you're just about in the right place to do something exciting.'

Following a whim can be as simple as changing our mind or experiencing something unusual. Have a conversation, either with someone you know well or with a stranger. Change your working location from the living room to the kitchen so that you see something different. Change your route to the office, and stop at this garden, look at that bird. We can routinely change our routine, adding or subtracting new habits, trying something new each month. Being whimsical mimics the unpredictable nature of our days and requires we step into the world in a new way, inviting more experience into our lives as a result.

Of course, we can't expect to follow our whims day after day, chasing surprise after surprise, seeking constant novelty—our days would overwhelm us. But maybe following our whims can be a way to listen to ourselves a little more closely—to bump into our deeper wants. Perhaps we can scrap the to-do list for a day—or even for an hour—and notice what we feel like doing, rather than what we should do. We can follow a whim without judgement and make sure we leave space for a surprise to find us—even when we least expect it. As the author Daniel Klein wrote, 'Even in the worst of times something usually comes along that spritzes me with hope—some small, everyday event that unexpectedly revives my appetite for life.'

When we let go of expectations and allow our deeper wants to surprise us, we might just start to notice the moments and people that spritz us with hope. Perhaps we can even start to collect these deeper wants to serve as reminders of how to feel good in our days, how to feel an aliveness—rather than continue to disappoint our great expectations. This way, a day becomes more than a list of shoulds: it can be a container for what we truly want. Better yet, perhaps it's a container with the lid off—one where we can discover new wants, where we can change our mind, where we can stretch but not fall.

When we want to do something, rather than feel we ought to, there's an inherent appreciation that can spill over into other parts of our lives—we can want, and also be content with what we have. Perhaps that's the antidote to tripping over our expectations. As the ancient Greek philosopher Epicurus said, 'Do not spoil what you have by desiring what you have not; remember that what you have now was once among the things you only hoped for.' Maybe we are looking through the wrong end of the telescope, fixating on what we expect for the future, rather than valuing what we have today. Not all days will be filled with our deepest wants and whimsy, with ladybugs crawling over us as we lie on the grass. That would be another expectation—to think that the things we want will simply come our way or our days will always be whimsical. There are happy accidents, but there are unhappy ones too. Our to-do list will fill up with different shoulds before we remember to let go. But we can lightly hold our wishes for our future—and perhaps sometimes do away with them entirely, or forget which drawer we tucked them in. We can focus on what we want to do, even if that's just being kind, instead of what we ought to do. We can plan to keep our options open and go with the flow until we decide to make plans. Not planning can become our plan, which might allow us to embrace uncertainty and see what unfolds for us.

As I remember hearing from a 90-year-old woman named Margaret, 'You can't arrange life; it happens around you.' When we try too hard to arrange life, there is less life for us to arrange. We may not be able to control the things that happen around us. But when we allow for what is in this day, we may just find it exceeds our expectations.

10

The Trap of Busyness

Wisely, and slow. They stumble that run fast.
William Shakespeare, *Romeo and Juliet*

If we spent a day collecting the answers we hear to the question 'How are you?', we wouldn't be wrong in thinking 'busy' has become synonymous with 'good'. We both project and presume busyness with the phrases 'I'm so busy', or 'I know you're so busy'. Instead of sharing what's novel, what we might need, or what's concerning us, we can use 'busy' as a stand-in for what's really going on in our daily and inner lives.

When the response to how we are isn't 'busy', often it's a close relative: 'I feel like I'm not doing enough.' When we perceive we don't measure up to our own expectations of busy, we experience productivity guilt. *Everyone else appears to be busy*, we think, *and here I am in the midst of my day, not quite busy enough, but not quite able to step into the room of rest while the pressure to be busy follows me around.* At times, busyness is unavoidable. Everything might come at once, or there's more and more added to our plate. Busyness may stem from making ends meet. We might have multiple and even conflicting responsibilities, pressing demands or unexpected events bogarting our days, making it difficult to untangle from being busy and still keep afloat in life.

Other times, busyness can be tied to coping with the day—during challenging times, some people take on more simply as a way of keeping moving. Busyness can be a buffer, just as retreating can be, allowing us to grieve or face something on our timeline.

Sometimes, we embrace busyness. We enjoy the sense of momentum it brings to our days. The adage 'If you want something done, ask a busy person' speaks to this. Work, multiple creative projects and a full social calendar can give shape to a day. Or perhaps it's simply our natural frequency to be busy, and to dampen it would mean dampening ourselves. But there is a distinct difference between the busy that is unavoidable, a comforting buffer or for our own momentum, and the needless busying that can perpetuate productivity guilt. That is, the busyness we wear as a badge of honour. For many in privileged circumstances, this busyness for its own sake is a choice, yet we rush around as if we have no say in the matter. We're just *so busy*—but to what end? As Ralph Waldo Emerson wrote in his journals, 'It is not enough to be busy; so are the ants. The question is: What are we busy about?' What are we so busy doing? Things we could delegate, things we could skip, things we could decline—things we do just for the sake of doing things? We rarely pause to think of how our days could be different without all the needless busying. It can sometimes be difficult to distinguish which variety of busyness we are entangled in. Perhaps the clue is that we feel we are in a tangle of our own making. Such self-imposed busyness often stems from a place of relentless ambition, comparison to others or expectation. *I should take on extra work so I can secure a promotion. I should take up a hobby—everyone on the internet is sharing theirs. I should fill my planner a month in advance so I don't have to face an empty day.*

Perhaps we are afraid that we if don't keep ourselves busy, the well will run dry. Sometimes we have a scarcity mindset—we say yes to every opportunity and invitation for fear it might be the last. Perhaps we even strive to be less busy, but find we are more admired or respected when we are keeping up the busyness charade, so we stay on the hamster wheel to keep up appearances.

Of course, this variety of busy is not entirely self-propelled— there is a pervasive societal pressure to have something to show for our time. An overworked lifestyle has become a status symbol: we conflate being busy with being important because society has taught us to.

We've internalised the idea that to be content, we must always be doing something—we need to be busy in order to be productive, successful or worthy. In turn, we've become over-reliant on being busy as it provides reassurance that our lives are moving, and therefore meaningful. But if we're perpetually caught in a cycle of doing more, we can be too busy to enjoy life.

Needless busyness, in this way, is an affliction. The academic Omid Safi shared this observation in an essay for The On Being

Project called 'The Disease of Being Busy': 'This disease of being "busy" (and let's call it what it is, the dis-ease of being busy, when we are never at ease) is spiritually destructive to our health and wellbeing. It saps our ability to be fully present with those we love the most in our families, and keeps us from forming the kind of community that we all so desperately crave.' Filling our days with the dis-ease of doing upon doing doesn't necessarily constitute time well spent—sometimes it's just a distraction from another dis-ease: that of figuring out what we really want to be doing with our days. We crowd our schedules with so much that we don't have time for the things that are most important to us. We become afraid of blank space and we turn away from rest, even though at times that's exactly what we need. We find ourselves saying yes to extraneous work or activities, either as a knee-jerk reaction or because it's a way to avoid doing the things that matter most to us.

This needless busyness can be one of the greatest stumbling blocks to attending to the fulfilling thing. It's perhaps no wonder— it's easier to attend to something that has a deadline than to something limitless and unstructured. It can seem more pressing to attend to someone else's needs, wants or demands than to our own wishes, pursuits and dreams. It can be less daunting to attend to the things we feel confident doing than to the things we are unsure about. It seems simpler to begin the things that have some semblance of certainty than to step into the great unknown.

While we may recognise that such busyness is our block, it can still be difficult to untangle ourselves from it. Modern life will continue to place busyness on a pedestal because it's profitable. In fact, capitalism has designed our busy lives for us. The increasing hours of the typical workday make free time scarce, increasing the likelihood that we'll pay a lot more for a convenient way to cheer ourselves up, to reward ourselves, to celebrate, to fix problems, to alleviate boredom if we have the means.

This scarcity of free time can contribute to productivity pressure: we have so little discretionary time available that we feel we must not waste it. Fulfilling but non-essential activities start to feel like a waste of time—reading, going for a walk, pottering in the garden, snuggling on the couch with a lover. Perhaps it's no coincidence that these are the very things that don't cost a thing. The best things in life might be free, but we don't have the time for them. When the equation is flipped—we earn less and have more time—the guilt can soften. We might not question spending an afternoon wandering around because we have the time.

But few of us can simply decide to earn less in order to work less. It can be difficult to unwind from the trappings of a busy world—especially if we're contending with financial precarity, or have dependants, or are focusing on a long-term goal. Some may not wish to—again, busyness can be what provides some people with momentum and even contentment. But for those of us who lament being busy and could find ways to be less so, why don't we? What prevents those of us who can afford to be less busy from finding something extraneous to dial down in our days? Why are we waiting for some time in the future to slow down if we could slow down now? What keeps propelling us to earn more to buy things we don't need or have the time to enjoy because we're *so busy*? Not all of us are in a position to contemplate such questions, but for those who are: in what area of your life is your busyness a choice? Where are you caught on the hamster wheel of doing more, earning more, striving more? Where are you conflating being busy with being good?

Perhaps we can't all dial down our busy, but we can come up with new answers to the question 'How are you?'—because when our knee-jerk response is 'busy', it can be a barrier to connection. When I spoke to the Australian social researcher Hugh Mackay, he said that busyness is a way to insulate ourselves from one another. 'It can be a way of not having to exercise compassion because we are distancing ourselves from the people that we could show compassion towards, where busyness is kind of the ultimate form of self-absorption in a way.'

Surely we don't want to be so busy that we don't have the time to connect with people. Surely we don't wish to be so busy that we don't enjoy our lives. Surely we don't *really* think busy is good— we just needed the permission from each other to be something else. After all, *busy* is not the same as *productive*, and *productive* is not the same as *worthwhile*.

The road to burnout

Busyness can be a prelude to burnout—the deflating and depleting condition that's hard to define, but is currently defining generations.

Whether it's a demanding work schedule or the looming threat of climate change, the sheer vastness of everything we need to do can feel overwhelming. At times, the number of things we think we should be doing—in our days and to save the world—feels impossible. There are just not enough hours in the day. Tasks that should take only a few minutes can stretch into hours, while other work mounts up.

The result? We feel exhausted. Our inaction as a result only increases our anxiety, perpetuating the feeling of being constantly overwhelmed. When we think about everything we have to do, we can feel weary before we even begin. Other times, we might get through our to-do list, only to find there's more to do waiting at the bottom of it. We have no gas left in the tank, but feel guilty stopping. Life becomes a ceaseless frenzy in which we always feel like we should be doing more just to keep up with everybody else—who all seem to be coping fine.

Hiding our burnout can perpetuate burnout in others. All too often, when we're feeling threadbare we do feel alone. We rarely glimpse the truth: that others are flailing too. Everybody just seems busy but somehow still upbeat. *Is there something wrong with me because I can't push through, pep up, work harder?* Conversely, we can lap it up when people assume we're busy, or admire how much we get done—but behind the scenes we're exhausted, too.

Just as the sources of burnout are many—an infectious pressure to be busy, for instance, or the precarious or uncertain nature of work, or troubling external events and circumstances—so are our experiences of it. The two-phase description by the writer Honor Eastly has long stuck with me: crispy and burned out. The crispy phase precedes burnout, and occurs when Honor is stretching herself but still enjoying the process. Perhaps it's a state of flow, or the motivation for the project is fuelling long hours. But there's a risk—you're moving but starting to catch on fire. The second phase comes when movement grinds to a halt—you feel stifled and burned.

This two-phase framing for burnout helped me recognise burnout amnesia in myself—the tendency to forget that if I keep running when I'm on fire, I might get burned. It's helped me recognise my own signals of crispiness before I land all the way in phase two: waking up at three in the morning worrying about a crowded to-do list, an intolerance of mess and noise, feeling alone, despondency, ruminating on what other people think. When I spot these signals, I can turn to the things that might help me cool off—asking others for help, taking deep breaths, exercising, resting, switching on an auto-email responder.

While this approach can be helpful to spot the warning signs, burnout can still blindside us. This might stem from the narrow definition of what we consider to be 'work'. Raising children, for example, isn't often considered 'real work', as it should be. So too taking care of an elderly parent. Even creative pursuits are denigrated in this way. This perpetuates our feeling of not doing enough, because what we do supposedly doesn't count.

Even on those days when I do feel on top of the administration of life, I berate myself for not doing enough. It's easy to overlook the fact that getting through the day can be work, as there's a constant stream of tasks: shopping for groceries, cooking and cleaning, paperwork for that insurance claim, phone calls to make, laundry to fold, news to check, entertainment to curate or create. Simply put, it takes time to be a human sustaining themselves—and that's before we add the work of the week, sustaining other humans, a second job, a fulfilling creative pursuit, the things we want to do in this life.

When we don't count the work of living as work, we can quickly reach exhaustion and have no idea why. At the end of our tether but not realising it, we wonder why such simple things feel both urgent and impossible. Responding to a text message is overwhelming.

A gentle request feels like an unthinkable demand. Mopping the floor would be a nightmare. Add a layer of shame, and the conclusion is that our ineptitude must be to blame.

More likely, the reason we can't get the supposedly simple things done isn't because we're particularly lazy, undisciplined or incompetent, but rather we're perpetually burned out. Familiar with this feeling, journalist Anne Helen Petersen described the phenomenon as errand-paralysis in her conversation-shifting *Buzzfeed* article 'How Millennials Became the Burnout Generation'. 'Why can't I get this mundane stuff done?' she asked. 'Because I'm burned out. Why am I burned out? Because I've internalized the idea that I should be working all the time. Why have I internalized that idea? Because everything and everyone in my life has reinforced it—explicitly and implicitly—since I was young.'

If we have internalised the idea that we should be busy all the time, or see no escape from the busyness of daily life, how do we find any reprieve from the consequent burnout? It's tempting to turn to a productivity hack or a new system to organise our lives, but these are like bandaids if we don't address our collective resistance to what we need most: rest.

Rest is not a moral failing

When our days get busier, many of us turn to doing more to keep up—we wake up earlier to get things done, we skip lunch, we stay late at work to catch up, or we delay sleep to regain some of the hours that seemed to slip away during the day.

Even if we know we should rest, we can find ourselves in a limbo where we are not working because we're exhausted, but we're not resting because we're stressed—and we wind up feeling bad about all of it. We've become accustomed to ignoring our need for rest so we can stay on top of things. We've divorced ourselves from what our bodies require—we feel we have to justify our tiredness, or check our to-do lists to see if we've done enough or can squeeze more in, placing that above the call of our bodies.

But the gains—if any—we might make in playing catch-up are short-lived. When we keep doing more to keep up, we only wind up feeling exhausted, stressed and burned out—and, perhaps unsurprisingly, we're less productive. As the consultant and author of *Rest: Why You Get More Done When You Work Less* Alex Soojung-Kim Pang told me in an interview, 'Generally, short bursts of long hours do lead to increases in productivity, but over time those gains disappear. The odds of costly mistakes rise, and as a result the gains that come from working longer hours disappear.'

Perhaps we resist rest not because we can't find the time, but because we fear the boredom that can accompany doing nothing. But boredom is an important part of our lives. Often it's used as a catch-all for feeling frustrated or upset or unfocused, but true boredom can be an important signal that something does not feel meaningful. As the researcher and philosophy professor Andreas Elpidorou wrote in a journal article titled 'The Bright Side of Boredom', 'In the absence of boredom, one would remain trapped in unfulfilling situations, and miss out on many rewarding experiences. Boredom is both a warning that we are not doing what we want to be doing and a "push" that motivates us to switch goals and projects.'

What are we missing by being so busy that we don't have time to rest or to be bored? While boredom can feel uncomfortable, we crave those moments of mind-wandering because they allow us to notice and exhale. What would we notice if we allowed ourselves to be bored from time to time? When we allow ourselves to be bored, we might be able to solve those very frustrations that we were mistaking for boredom. We can seek boredom by making space in our days to simply be with ourselves or have an aimless conversation.

When our culture is pushing us into a spiral of busyness, rest may be the only thing that helps keep us intact. Rest shouldn't be for the sole purpose of making us more productive—it has value in and of itself. It reminds us that we are not machines, but human beings. When we embrace rest or take what is within reach for us—be it a guilt-free nap or a sabbatical—we can demonstrate the value to others, too.

So how do we find it? Maybe if we've long resisted rest because we experience productivity guilt, anxiety or shame, it might first be helpful to think again of the sponge metaphor—the absorb is what enables the squeeze. Productivity often has less to do with the number of hours we squeeze out of the working day, and more to do with our energy, focus and attention—making rest an essential part of the equation. Productivity, in the true sense of the word, is composed of far more than busyness—it's formed from a variety of elements in our life: from sleeping well, taking a break, moving around, and alternating between focus and break.

I often have to remind myself that while I could keep trudging along in my day, hunched over with an exhaustion that I will doubtless take into tomorrow, I'd be better off if I rested today in order to refresh. Allowing myself to be horizontal for a while is the one thing that helps me spring upright again. Even if it's not quite restoration, I can at least count on having a new-found impetus to do the thing (either because of the nudge that less time brings or because I have more energy now that I'm rested), rather than carrying the same grind into a new day.

Sometimes, having a horizontal day isn't a conscious choice—our mental and physical health can give us no choice but to rest, without the assurance of a spring in our step after. But for those of us who do have a choice—why don't we take rest when we can?

Part of the challenge of working less is that we're entrenched in a system that demands more and more, but it might also be true that we've been taught to resist rest. Even the weekend has fallen victim to our need to avoid rest—through devoting time to a side hustle, or dashing between social catch-ups, the hours hurtle by until we greet the 'Sunday scaries' and wonder where our chance to rest went. In her book *The Weekend Effect*, Katrina Onstad wrote about the benefits of taking time off and how, amid a culture of overwork, we should protect our right to a weekend. 'Whether it's motivated by the push of business or the pull of the soul (or some combination of the two), two days off is what feels normal and human. After hundreds of years of debate, bloodshed, and dogma, a weekend should be an enshrined right—yet that isn't exactly what happened. It took a century to win the weekend. It's taken only a few decades to undo it.'

Having a work-free weekend—or even taking a break—has almost become a lost art. Even when we know we need rest and have the privilege to take it, it can be difficult to convince ourselves to do nothing—without also having a side of self-flagellation.

Perhaps it's all in the framing—both from society, but also from the environments we grow up in. This clicked for me when I spoke with psychotherapist and author Hilary Jacobs Hendel about emotions. On the topic of productivity guilt, she explained that whether we feel ease or resistance towards rest has a lot to do with how it was modelled for us when we were growing up. If your weekends as a kid were spent relaxing on the couch, for example, you might have an easier time leaning into rest as an adult—whereas if it was all go-go-go, you might well feel like you're being lazy if you don't keep up that intensity.

For those of us who feel unease at doing nothing, perhaps we need to lean the other way—into the lazy. Maybe it's worth inspecting why we bring negative connotations towards laziness, and inspect what circumstances, situations or ideas lie beneath our judgements of it. Are we really being lazy, or have we internalised the idea that we should be working all the time? Are we really being lazy, or did we have a terrible night's sleep? Are we really being lazy, or are we contending with ill-health, a poor financial situation, an overwhelming schedule? Are we really being lazy, or do we just not want to do the thing—and maybe we don't have to?

Instead of lumping together our varying circumstances and the root causes of our behaviour in the category of laziness, perhaps it needs its time in the spotlight. What if we wore a good night's sleep, an afternoon nap, taking a sick day, or a weekend spent enjoying the sweetness of nothing as a badge of honour?

What if being lazy or slothful was our aspiration, rather than busyness? According to the zoologist, author and explorer Lucy Cooke, taking lessons from sloths could help save us and the planet.

In her TED Talk titled 'Sloths! The Strange Life of the World's Slowest Mammal', Cooke shared how we can learn a lot from the ingenious adaptations of this misunderstood creature. 'How about we all embrace our inner sloth by slowing down, being more mindful, reducing wasteful convenience, being economical with our energy, recycling creatively and reconnecting with nature,' she said. 'Otherwise, I fear, it will be us humans that turn out to be "the stupidest animals that can be found in the world".'

Slowing down to rest isn't a moral failing—it's essential to help us recharge and reflect. As Hugh Mackay told me, being human is an undeniably demanding business, so we all need a break. 'I think we have to build into every day some time that's just for us. It's not selfish; it is self-replenishing.'

Viewing rest as self-replenishing rather than selfish might help ease the guilt or shame some of us feel for taking a break, and instead help us to see that it's part of the rhythm of the day. It also shifts the frame so we see the inherent value of rest—we need it to restore and replenish, but also to rethink. The trap we can find ourselves in is that we are too busy to rest, and so we don't have the time to rethink our circumstances and come up with another way to be. Rest might be the key to releasing us from the busyness trap, because it's the very thing that can help us see we're in it.

To allow ourselves more rest, we can perhaps broaden our idea of it so we can find what is within our reach, depending on our circumstances but also our preferences. Rest can take different forms—it doesn't have to be an expensive retreat or ten-step self-care ritual. The way we experience rest varies from person to person, as does the type of rest each of us needs. In her TED Talk 'The Real Reason We Are Tired and What to Do About It', Dr Saundra Dalton-Smith talks about how we have incorrectly combined the concepts of sleep and rest, when sleep is simply one of the seven types of rest we need: physical, mental, sensory, creative, emotional, social and spiritual.

We can determine the rest we need by looking at where we are using most of our energy in the day. Perhaps rest for you is getting more sleep. Or maybe it is walking in nature, a morning of solitude, playing an instrument or watching the clouds pass by. I rather like going to a local grocer's, to unhurriedly wander the aisles of fruits and vegetables and return home to make a soup—for someone else, of course, this might be the opposite of restful.

Giving yourself permission to rest in the way you need it can be the very thing that allows you to discover more opportunities to shape your day, rather than having busyness shape it for you. Taking things slow and slothful can help us survive. So find the beauty in the break. Enjoy that moment of boredom. Be okay with what is left undone. Allow yourself to rest, pause, ponder, daydream, laze, do nothing. Listen, watch and reflect, and embrace the possibilities of not being busy.

Maybe don't do the thing

Often we find ourselves hanging on to the illusion of a calmer and more manageable next week when things will settle down, only to find ourselves faced with another crammed schedule. Instead of waiting for everything around us to stop, what if we simply stopped in the middle of everything? While the COVID-19 pandemic has had different impacts on different people, at certain points we learned what it means to stop—stop commuting, stop making too many social commitments, stop endlessly travelling for work, stop overcommitting on our weekends. For some of us, this meant that we stopped being *so busy*. Granted, some people were even busier. There no doubt remains a collective grief for loved ones, for our communities and for our lives as they once were—but there was also a quiet hope that maybe things could look different. While acknowledging that the world shutting down had devasting impacts on many people, as well as on parts of our own lives, there were often whispers of relief that we didn't have to do the thing we didn't want to do after all.

Maybe we don't need a forced stop to give ourselves permission to slow down. We're taught that if we don't grind, then we don't get. But what are we seeking to get? Is it what we actually want? Might we be okay if we don't have to do the thing to get another thing, and we could just be?

Things won't settle down until we settle them down on a societal level. The trajectory of busyness will continue until we make a swift change—or, as we saw, until a pandemic jams the hamster wheel. So what can we do individually? Perhaps we can create that stop for ourselves at different times, for different things. When I interviewed the jeweller Sarah Jane Adams, she spoke about how every couple of years she will purposefully hit the reset button on her life to get a blank slate. The consequence, in her words, is that it opens new horizons: 'New things come into your life. It's clearing all the things that don't work for you, all the things that you've become comfortable with.'

When we resist hitting the reset button, things can begin to deteriorate, including ourselves. Sarah encouraged me when I told her about a project that I was thinking of stopping: 'Do it, otherwise you're going to have to soak it in antiseptic. It's going to turn infected and it will be awful. Just rip it off. Do it, because as soon as you do it, as soon as you get rid of all of that, you will breathe.' She was right. I let go of the project, and even though I felt I was disappointing other people, I felt lighter. New things came to me once I made the space, just as Sarah had assured me they would.

It doesn't have to be a grand stop to help us figure out what's important to us—we can practise putting down books we are no longer enjoying, or stopping midway through a sentence of a report you're writing that can wait until tomorrow. When we don't do the thing for a while, we might find that it's not as important as we thought—the world keeps turning, the wheels don't fall off, and we learn a valuable lesson: we may not have to remain in this fug of busyness.

Stopping can bring clarity, but it can also bring pleasure. A study on consumption experiences by the American Marketing Association found that when a pleasurable activity is interrupted, it is rendered more pleasurable when we recommence it. Whether we're listening to a song, sitting in a massage chair or taking a bite of a meal, a well-timed pause can prevent us from becoming numb to the pleasure.

Sacrificing something for a short period can also reset your senses. When I spoke to Annie Raser-Rowland, the co-author of *The Art of Frugal Hedonism*, she talked about experimenting with the reset effect in our daily life. Perhaps we eat only the humblest of home cooking for a week, so that when you next taste a mango it's like it dances on your tongue. We can reset our relationship to technology by having a screen-free 24 hours. We can reset our calendars by cancelling plans so we consider more carefully when to say yes and when to say no.

So often we feel obliged to squeeze as much as we can into each day, ignoring the harmful toll it can take on our bodies, on our relationships, and even on the very thing we are striving to propel forward but are too busy to attend to. We forget that we can politely decline, we can reset, and that there may be less to do than we pretend.

Maybe we can't cancel our plans or stop doing certain things, but we can experiment with not adding more to the list. As the writer and entrepreneur David Cain said, 'What if, for a whole year, you stopped acquiring new things or taking on new pursuits. Instead, you return to abandoned projects, stalled hobbies, unread books and other neglected intentions, and go deeper with them than you ever have before.'

How far we extend the experiment of stopping depends on our situation, but in whatever big or small ways we can pause the doing, it may enliven us to the myriad choices we have in our days about what we take on. Do we really need to add to our to-do list just because we got through it? Do we really need to schedule every moment of our children's time? Do we really need to take on an extra project, or cram to finish something over the weekend? Can't it wait? Can we go deeper instead of always trying to spread ourselves so thin? Instead of being caught on the hamster wheel, maybe we can simply hop off. Maybe there is something to taking things slower, not chasing after every opportunity, not feeling overwhelmed by our own ambitions, perfection or expectations that keep us busy. Maybe we need to cultivate more praise for being right where we are, rather than continually looking ahead.

Perhaps the same goes not just for our own health, but for the planet's. We don't need more needlessly busy people, but more people who can slow down and step into what they can offer where they are—people who can pause, who can step off the hamster wheel, who can demonstrate that it's okay not to keep up with the Joneses.

Society and the environment might be better off if there were more of us producing less and consuming less. For those who have the privilege to choose to be busy or to stop, perhaps it's the pause that is most important—again, we can take a lesson from the sloth and slow down. There's no guarantee our individual efforts will slow down the speed of the world or the destruction of it—and relatively powerless individuals are not to blame for not making 'better' environmental choices, for example, when outrage and accountability should lie with the powerful—but we might discover a side effect nevertheless: a sense of purpose in our days, doing our bit.

We can live lightly when it comes to what we consume, as well as live light-heartedly in all areas of our lives. We can notice when less may be more, go deeper into one task rather than spreading ourselves thinly across several, and only add something new to our to-do list when we've checked off something else.

If we experiment with just stopping, with politely declining the opportunity for more, we might find it makes us more creative, more curious, more content—and we might not be so afraid of what we'll find in stillness, boredom and rest. And, valuably, by doing so in our own lives, we might signal to others that it's okay for them to stop too. Instead of busy, we can feel free. And perhaps that's it—perhaps, when asked how we are, we should aim to answer: 'Free.'

11

The Denial of Limitation

*I can never read all the books I want. I can never be all the people
I want and live all the lives I want. I can never train myself in all
the skills I want. And why do I want? I want to live and feel all the
shades, tones, and variations of mental and physical experience as
possible in my life. And I am horribly limited.*

Sylvia Plath, *The Unabridged Journals of Sylvia Plath*

Perhaps you didn't do the thing today because there are limits to
what can be done in a day.

When we greet each day, we are greeting its limitation—the
limited hours in a working day, our limited free time, our limited
energy and resources. Yet we can often place expectations on
ourselves and our days as if these limitations don't exist—we can
set sky-high ambitions, take on countless responsibilities and make
plans upon plans.

When the things we need or ought to do keep spilling over into tomorrow, we may turn to optimising our days—if we adopt a new time-management technique, we think, we'll finally get on top of things. But the promises of optimisation deny our limitations, when we might be better off embracing them. With limitations on our time, energy, money, motivation, health and attention, we cannot expect that we will attend to everything—we'll only exhaust ourselves, or others, in trying. Sometimes we just won't fit the thing in today.

Recognising our limitations might seem defeatist, but I think there's meaning to be found in not getting everything done. We shouldn't want to be able to get to everything we want to do—surely we should want there to be more in life than we'll ever be able to grasp. If we reach the point where we've checked every box, life might be complete—but it would also be over. Limitations make life worth living.

It can be both a relief and a motivation to be reminded of the fact that we're not going to get everything done, or even most things. As I learned from journalist Oliver Burkeman, facing our limitations isn't about accepting a lower standard for our lives, but rather bringing into our conscious awareness a limitation that we already have. 'Once we recognise that there is no way to optimise ourselves into being perfect, hyper-productive beings,' he said, 'we can actually get on with spending our limited time and using our limited resources for what matters to us most.'

We might be 'horribly limited', as Sylvia Plath put it, but it's part and parcel of being alive. There are limits to our days, and limits to ourselves—how much we can change, how much we can do. It reminds us that our days are finite and therefore precious.

A day rarely feels long enough for everything we want to do. There is always more pressing on us than it is possible to accomplish, and that can be what propels us. We won't get on top of it all—and we can miss what's actually happening in our lives if we fixate on trying to squeeze everything in.

A container for the fulfilling things

When we're behind, late or struggling to stay on top of things, the message we might receive from others, or have internalised, is that we just don't know how to prioritise.

But what if prioritising is a challenge precisely because there are so many things in our life that are a priority? Priorities aren't distributed evenly—some of us can pick and choose what's most pressing, while others have many things thrust upon us. Limitations are the same—they can vary from person to person, day by day. We see this in how the hours in the day are not available for each of us in the same way—we may work nine-to-five, care for young children, pile one gig upon another or have the flexibility of freelancing. We also see this with the influence money has and the variances it can introduce into our days. As Eula Biss wrote in *Having and Being Had*, not having money can be time-consuming. 'There are hours spent at laundromats, hours at bus stops, hours at free clinics, hours at thrift stores, hours on the phone with the bank or the credit-card company or the phone company over some fee, some little charge, some mistake.'

Prioritising systems can further perpetuate our urge to self-blame. I've come to see such systems or hacks as different from recognising our priorities in life. Prioritising systems promise control, where our priorities can reveal what's important to us. Where prioritising promises a cure-all, knowing our priorities can guide us to what works for us.

So perhaps rather than leaping into making a list of priorities, we can identify the limitations in our day and discover our priorities within them. The creator of the popular blog *Wait But Why*, Tim Urban, shared a helpful approach to visualising the limitation of time in his article '100 Blocks a Day'. Factoring in that most people sleep around seven or eight hours each night, that leaves us with sixteen or seventeen hours awake each day, or around 1000 minutes. Urban represented these as 100 ten-minute blocks. 'Throughout the day, you spend ten minutes of your life on each block, until you eventually run out of blocks and it's time to go to sleep,' he wrote.

Placing the blocks into a ten-by-ten grid, we can then label each to gain insight into how we are spending them. 'How many of them are put towards making your future better, and how many of them are just there to be enjoyed?' Urban asked. 'How many of them are spent with other people, and how many are for time by yourself? How many are used to create something, and how many are used to consume something? How many of the blocks are focused on your body, how many on your mind, and how many on neither one in particular? Which are your favourite blocks of the day, and which are your least favourite?'

We have a finite number of blocks in a day and in our lifetime. Sometimes it takes seeing our limited number laid out before us to make us step back and consider how we are spending each one.

There is, of course, a flipside to seeing our time limitations in this way. Focusing on our blocks might add pressure to our days. We might obsess over filling each one, or worry about the blocks we have wasted, and once again find ourselves falling down the 'if only' spiral. But it would be unrealistic to think we can seize every ten-minute block in our days—yes, they are limited, but so is our capacity to fill them perfectly. Once again, acknowledging that we can't do everything in a day allows us to focus on what we did do—we can look back on our 100 blocks, and instead of saying, 'I only did two blocks of exercise today,' we can say, 'I already did two blocks of exercise.'

To account for our human fallibility and the days that go off track, I think we need 'buffer blocks'. There will be days we need more sleep, days our commute takes longer than usual, days we battle a migraine, days there is an emergency of some kind, days we obsess over a personal quandary. The thing about priorities is that they are constantly shuffling, depending on what's most important to us in the moment.

Other times, there will be days we think we can't possibly fit more in, but then we find ourselves meeting a date for a spontaneous lunchtime stroll. We fit it in because we *want* to fit it in. When tragedy or crisis strikes, people pause what they are doing and rally around—suddenly the meeting or deadline doesn't matter as much as being there for others. There's a romance to be found in spontaneity in all its forms—in embracing what a block was filled with, rather than dwelling on what we thought it should have been. We have to account for the unexpected in all its forms: we need to be okay with rearranging our blocks, because life will always rearrange them for us.

Perhaps, with this in mind, acknowledging our limitations is less about trying to optimise each minute of the day, but rather creating more space to account for the variances we will encounter.

Perhaps each of us has things that take up our blocks that really don't need to be there. This is where the 100 blocks exercise can help us find where there is some flexibility contained in our limited days—whatever that looks like for each of us. Maybe we start meal-prepping on a Sunday instead of cooking each night. Maybe we spend Saturday mornings on a creative project rather than meeting friends for brunch. Maybe it's the nudge we needed to leave a job, relationship or city. This is all contingent on other limitations we may face in our days—and it's important not to compare our set of 100 blocks to others' blocks, but to focus on the flexibility in our own. We can accept, too, that the configuration of our 100 blocks will look different through our lives.

Rearranging our blocks in a way that works for us requires creativity—both to uncover where we might find empty blocks, and then in deciding how we fill them. This is something only we can define for ourselves. We should ask ourselves often: what is the fulfilling thing, and how do we arrange our blocks around it to create a container for it? Regularly returning to this question might help us assess if we are focusing on the right thing, instead of working hard at the wrong thing.

Filling one block with something takes away room for something else, so knowing what's important to us helps us decide which trade-offs make sense. As the academic Susan Carland told me, 'I have to keep reminding myself that every time I say yes to one thing, I'm saying no to something else—be it my kids, my job, or my sleep.'

Personally, I have a tendency to rush to say yes—I'm a people-pleaser—and I often find that this means I've said no to something important in my own life. I'm now learning to take some time to consider my limited blocks in a day before I reply to an invitation or request, and to make sure I'm allowing space for the fulfilling thing, whether that's rest, a creative project, exercise or time with someone I care for.

Even when we keep the 100 blocks at the forefront of our mind, it can still be difficult to protect them. It is often easier to say no to ourselves than to other people, especially if the reason to decline is because you simply want to reserve some blocks for yourself. While being quick to say yes can help us avoid disappointing others and open ourselves up to new opportunities, it can have a cost—we may wind up feeling resentful, overwhelmed, exhausted.

So we must be discerning. In learning to say no to certain things, we create space for saying yes to more fitting things. To guard space for what is important, I've found it helpful to create a blanket no rule—that is, I always gently decline certain things. When I first started out as a freelancer, for example, I was having a lot of morning coffee catch-ups with acquaintances, which I soon found were robbing me of essential writing time as my mind is sharpest in the morning. These days I never say yes to a morning coffee catch-up, which helps alleviate my people-pleaser guilt because it's a blanket rule, rather than personal.

The societal pressure to say yes means that it can take us a long time to feel comfortable saying no. Speaking to the writer Heather Havrilesky, I learned that we don't have to feel like terrible people for not wanting to do certain things—we can trust what's best for us. It might sound obvious, but it was life-changing for me to hear Heather's words: 'You can actually just say that's not really my thing. As long as you don't feel like you're cutting yourself off from everything, or you're too anxious to do anything, or you're living inside your fear all the time, you're not obligated to live someone else's idea of a good life. You are actually obligated to honour the kind of life that you want to live.' I now find it easier to say, 'Thank you, but I don't do coffee catch-ups,' or 'I'm not adding anything new to my to-do list until next month,' or 'That's not really my thing but thanks for thinking of me.' If all else fails, perhaps we can borrow the author E.B. White's approach. In a response to an invitation to join the committee of the Arts and Sciences for Eisenhower, he was thankful but said, 'I must decline, for secret reasons.' That may be as good a reason as any.

Perhaps, by being mindful of our own limited blocks, we can be mindful of those of others, too. How are you asking things of other people? Could you be more generous or flexible? Are you considering their current circumstances? Might there be alternatives? Do you make space for someone to politely decline? By asking with more generosity and the option to decline, we can begin to normalise saying no—which gives each of us more space to fill our days with what's important to us, rather than with unnecessary obligations.

Creating limitations to do the important things
Overlooking our limitations is a recipe for feeling overwhelmed— we can easily create limitless to-do lists, fooling ourselves into thinking we are juggling multiple things successfully, when in fact we aren't attending to anything well.

But limitations can work in our favour—indeed, it's much better to work with our limitations than against them. We see this clearly

in the creative process—it's our limitations, not infinite possibility, that can lead to novel ideas. Without constraints, research has
found, complacency sets in and we follow what psychologists call the
path of least resistance. We tend to rely on obvious solutions, rather
than investing in the development of better ideas. Constraints—in
time, scope or resources—can provide the boundaries we need to
connect the dots.

In other words, if there were no box, we couldn't think outside
it, or know when to push against it. It's a bit like a fence at the edge
of a cliff—with that in place, you can explore the pasture freely
without worrying about falling off the edge. Without the fence,
you might plant yourself the middle of the field, playing it safe, and
overlook possibilities and new discoveries.

While too many constraints—like a micromanager—can be stifling, they can prove helpful on the days we need to do the important
things instead of roaming aimlessly. Here are some approaches I've
found useful to utilise the advantages of limitations.

Make your limitations tangible

While our list of things to do can be endless, what we can do in any
given time is limited. Consider using something like the Kanban
system—a visual way of managing tasks and workflows that utilises
an analogue or digital board with columns and cards. In its simplest
form, you create three columns to categorise tasks: to do, doing,
and done. Having an overview of all tasks and stages is a tangible
way to decide what to do next in the time you have.

There are two key limitations built into the system. The first is
that you can have a maximum of three tasks in the middle 'doing'

column at any given time. Before adding another, you must either complete a task (and then move it to the 'done' column) or abandon it, which helps to minimise the fatigue caused by switching tasks.

The second restriction is that the scope of any task is limited. Each item must be small and achievable, so it doesn't become a barrier to beginning. Over time, we learn to be more realistic about what we can achieve in a day—and then we can enjoy the smug feeling of moving a task from 'doing' to 'done'.

We may also learn that enough is as good as a feast. When we realise that not everything needs to be tied up with a bow at the end of the day, we can reflect on what we have achieved, rather than on what we haven't.

Start with the end in mind

A lot of emphasis gets placed on starting—'just do it', 'make it happen', 'don't wait for inspiration', 'begin now', 'start before you're ready'. But the key to starting, I've observed, is knowing when and how we'll finish. When we have an end point in sight, and can devise manageable steps to get there, starting becomes less daunting. For example, tell yourself you'll work on something for the next 45 minutes only and you likely won't feel pressured to work all day long. I like to mark the start and end of a timed writing session with a ding of a desk bell, creating an aural cue for myself to begin and finish.

Turn limitless oceans into puddles

Without limitations, the task at hand can become overwhelming. It's common for us to fixate on the whole, and to be overwhelmed by the sheer amount of work involved, or by the ever-expanding scope of our to-do list.

Thinking about everything we have to do all at once can leave us feeling stuck and stifled. We are looking at our to-do list as if it's a vast ocean, with no end in sight. It can bring a swell of anxiety that feels like a tidal wave. The antidote is something I like to call 'puddle theory'—a way to divide overwhelming tasks and take things smallest step by smallest step. Instead of contemplating the insurmountable sea, we can create tiny puddles that we don't fear stepping into, making it easier to begin. For example, instead of focusing on a disorderly garage we want to tidy, we can take the task item by item.

Puddle theory allows us to take on right-sized tasks, and even move between them—splashing about in one puddle may lead us unexpectedly to another. This is a helpful reminder that often it doesn't matter much where we start—what's important is the act of starting itself. The other puddles aren't going anywhere. In other words, focus on taking the first small step, and the others will seem more achievable in turn.

An important note is that puddle theory helps us recognise when one problem is actually several in disguise. I like to make a list of tasks and to-dos and then break tasks down into the smallest action possible. For example, 'start a podcast' becomes bite-sized tasks: make a list of guests, email a designer about cover art, buy a microphone, and so on. I'll then assign small actions to small pockets of time—typically 45 minutes each—and that's when I step into the puddle.

Puddle theory is a practice, and certainly not a cure-all, but by containing what we need to do, we become more realistic about what gets done in the limited time we have. Bit by bit, puddle by puddle, we wade through what was once overwhelming—and we may find ourselves content with small steps.

Engineer your own deadline

Perhaps there is no greater impetus to do the thing than an impending deadline—the countless assignments submitted a minute before the cut-off time are a testament to this. This is Parkinson's law in action, which suggests that work expands to fill the time available to us. If we have an entire day available to get something done, we will most likely use the whole day, probably including some idle time. If we only have an hour, we will likely seize that hour.

We can create our own deadlines in our days if we find we procrastinate without them—we can set a timer for a task, we can put a start or end date in a calendar, we can even ask a friend to check in with us once a week as a way to create a human deadline. I've come to recognise the reality that I'm an 'eleventh hour' kind of person and, with a little help from my friends, create a workaround. I have a few friends who I regularly meet with virtually or in person to tackle our 'puddles' together, 45 minutes at a time with my bell in tow!

Deadlines can also be applied to our life goals. When the artist Del Kathryn Barton was in her late teens, she gave herself a deadline to pursue her career as an artist. As she told me, 'I'm ambitious and the career aspect of my art practice has always been really important to me, so I created a set of goals and gave myself ten years to realise them. I said to myself that if I turn 30 and I haven't realised these things, then I would retrain in something else.'

Whatever the deadline you create, try to remember that you're human. Things may take twice as long as we think—even when we account for them taking twice as long. As Arnold Bennett wrote in *How to Live on 24 Hours a Day*, 'Beware of undertaking too much at the start. Be content with quite a little. Allow for accidents. Allow for human nature, especially your own.'

The awe and wonder of limitlessness

When we feel caught in the minutiae of our daily lives, or our lives feel like they're submerged in pointlessness, sometimes we need to consider the limitlessness of life, rather than its limits.

The ache of our limitations can subside when we look for awe and wonder in the world around us. We just have to look up, as the self-taught astronomer Greg Quicke reminded me. 'Often we think within our 10-foot radius that everything is happening to us. Step outside of that 10-foot radius and you'll frequently see that the same things are happening to others around you at the same time. Perhaps that can make it easier if we're able to see that it is not just all about us.'

We can spend so much of our days looking down into our phones, perhaps comparing ourselves to others. But when we look up and around us, we can find comfort in the idea that we're just one small person, nestled in something vast.

Sometimes, when I'm weary from the day or steeped in my own melancholia, I'll look up the image known as the Hubble Ultra Deep Field and feel the awe it inspires. The photograph was taken by a space telescope pointed at what appeared to be a blank piece of sky the size of a grain of sand. The ten-day exposure yielded a picture of over 10,000 galaxies in a tiny speck of the universe. When I ponder the image, I think to myself: *Here I am, a person, on this planet, in this solar system, in this galaxy we call the Milky Way, in the company of a limitless number of other galaxies. I am but a speck, on a speck, on a speck, on a speck—why agonise over what I did or didn't do when it doesn't matter as much as matter itself?*

Sitting with the limitlessness of the universe in this way can create what's termed the 'overview effect', and sometimes bring perspective to our worries, fears, undone tasks, shoulds and priorities. This perspective can also come from pondering the limitlessness of time. As the astronomer Carl Sagan put it in *Cosmos*, 'The lifetime of a human being is measured by decades, the lifetime of the Sun is a hundred million times longer. Compared to a star, we are like mayflies, fleeting ephemeral creatures who live out their lives in the course of a single day.'

We may never fully comprehend the scale of time and space— it's baffling to consider that if the history of the universe were compressed to a cosmic calendar year, humankind would only appear in the last few seconds on New Year's Eve—but we might for a moment be able to step outside our small-speck self and consider whether the worry is really worth it.

Of course, there are times when contemplating the vastness of the universe can lead us to a more nihilistic view: *If I am but a speck, and what I did or didn't do doesn't matter in the grand scheme of things, then why bother at all?* Perhaps, when zooming right out, we must remember to zoom right back in to where we live, right here, in this day. Who is to say this day isn't made for us to do what we believe matters? Maybe we are not an insignificant speck, but rather a miraculous one.

Perhaps the limitlessness of the universe can help us recognise the limitlessness in ourselves. While facing our limitations in our days can help us accept that we won't ever get everything done in our lifetime, it doesn't mean we have to place limiting views on ourselves—or abide by those placed upon us by others. In fact, I think embracing our limitations can be the very impetus to make us a little braver in our days—knowing that our time here is limited, we can remind ourselves to live as if we are limitless.

Sometimes we need to be limitless in our wants and ideas in order to get out of our own limiting mindsets. The work of the social psychologist Carol S. Dweck proves the adage true that when one door closes, another opens. In *Mindset: The New Psychology of Success*, Dweck explained the difference between having a fixed mindset about our character, intelligence and creative ability, and what's called a growth mindset.

'Believing that your qualities are carved in stone—the fixed mindset—creates an urgency to prove yourself over and over,' Dweck wrote. 'If you have only a certain amount of intelligence, a certain personality, and a certain moral character—well, then you'd better prove that you have a healthy dose of them. It simply wouldn't do to look or feel deficient in these most basic characteristics.'

On the other hand, a growth mindset is based on the belief that your basic qualities are things you can cultivate through your efforts and strategies, and with help from others. As Dweck explained, 'Although people may differ in every which way—in their initial talents and aptitudes, interests, or temperaments—everyone can change and grow through application and experience.'

When we cultivate a growth mindset, not only do we see more possibility in ourselves, but we also see the possibilities of the world around us. We stop defining something as a failure, and maybe even look forward to making the next courageous mistake.

When it doesn't matter in the grand scheme of things, then it also doesn't matter if we try for something and fail. Nor does it matter if something appears pointless or futile to somebody else, or whether we will ever quite reach what we're aiming for. We can do the thing anyway. As Emily Flake wrote in an essay for *McSweeney's* titled 'I Was in Charge of the Deck Chairs on the Titanic and They Absolutely Did Need Rearranging', 'Your efforts matter as much as they always did, which is to say not one little tiny bit, except that they are the most precious of things—they are your heart. Take care of your heart, my friends, and I shall see you on the other side.' What we do in this life, and the moments we seize, might not matter one iota, but they matter wholly because, at the end of the limited day, they are all we have. Life is finite, and yet many of us go on living day after day, not giving attention to the things that are most important to us, or marvelling at the awe of it all. We forget to take care of our heart, and bring our heart to the day. We forget we have but one opportunity to use it.

Our days will not always be filled with awe and wonder, but perhaps we can create small moments to bump against, that can help us reflect on our ultimate deadline. We can keep a coin in our pockets as a reminder to ask ourselves how we are spending our time. We can wear a watch and ask ourselves the same question when we feel it brush against something. We can take a stroll through a cemetery and remember the short time we have to walk through our days.

We can make a ritual of reflecting on our mortality each morning. The illustrator Maira Kalman is known for starting her days by reading the obituaries, this daily reminder of her own mortality serving as the ultimate wake-up call. As she told me, 'It makes you really conscious of the fact that you have a very limited amount of time. And within that time, the only thing that you can really do is to find what work is important to you.'

The work that is important to us is as varied as we are. But it's often that which might never appear on a résumé, but rather makes for a wonderful eulogy because it's the work of the heart. While it may seem morbid to reflect on what we want our own obituary to say—how we want our lives to be summarised at the end—there is motivation to be found in our mortality. It can help us find clarity, inspire us to do the things we want to do, and ensure that we don't become sidetracked by the pettiness of daily life—we can remember to be alive to life while we're still alive.

We move through our days as if we're in a holding pattern, waiting for our real lives to begin—waiting until we're on holiday to read all the books we want, until the children are grown or we retire to live the life we want, until we have more time to learn new skills. We go on as if we have all the tomorrows in the world, infinitely postponing our real life.

But this is it—this day, this life, is not a dress rehearsal for another. There's just the one show, and it's the most spectacular one we will ever get. So do the thing you want in spite of it all, and bring your heart to it, even if it's for a limited time only.

12

The Harsh Rules
of Discipline

Is not life a hundred times too short for us to bore ourselves?
Friedrich Nietzsche, *Beyond Good and Evil*

We tend to revere people who appear to be disciplined in their work, routines or habits, yet it's something many of us feel we lack. If only I were just more disciplined in my days, I often tell myself, perhaps I would be better. I'd be the kind of person who could stick to a routine, optimise my productivity, achieve balance, implement new habits perfectly and eliminate distractions with ease.

When we talk about discipline through the lens of productivity, we often couple it with unrelenting strictness, precise execution and perfect adherence to the rules we set ourselves. Being disciplined has punishment baked in—not only are the regimes or schedules punishing, but if we slip up, we will be reprimanded—either by someone else, or by our own guilty mind.

This punishing form of discipline can put undue pressure on the unpredictable nature of our days. We assume that sheer discipline will be enough to ride out any bumps we encounter, in our mood or in our environment, when in reality it can be a punishing expectation we're placing on ourselves. We need discipline—it helps us find order and regulation where there is none. But we also need to be flexible when we encounter the bumps. 'Without order, nothing can exist,' Oscar Wilde wrote in *The Picture of Dorian Gray*. 'Without chaos, nothing can evolve.'

While strict rules or consequences can be motivating for some, I find they more often bring a sense of dread to the things I want to do in my day. *Why does everything have to be difficult and punishing? Can't it be simple and pleasurable?* I believe we can find order in our days—and do the things we want to do—without the punishment of discipline.

Let's reassess the driver behind discipline. The philosopher Alan Watts also thought it was necessary to find a new word for the concept. Most people who taught a discipline, he argued in the lecture 'How to Enjoy Life', 'teach it with a kind of violence, as if a discipline was something that is going to be extremely unpleasant— something that you are going to have to put up with'.

As Watts explained, punishment is not the secret of discipline— it's not meant to be something we put up with, but rather a skill we cultivate. 'Discipline is a way of expression; say we want to express your feelings in stone. Now stone doesn't give way very easily, it is tough stuff. So you have to learn the skill of the discipline of the sculptor, in order to express yourself in stone.'

When we think of discipline as a skill—when we talk about 'a discipline' instead of 'being disciplined'—we couple it with interest, eagerness and the pleasure of learning. It has delight baked into it, rather than punishment. And delight can be a far more powerful motivation than punishment, strict rules or pressure. For many of the people I've interviewed, their creative practice was *a* discipline that brings delight, and didn't require a punishing schedule. We don't have to be pursuing a creative profession for the driver behind discipline to be creative. Perhaps taking a disciplined approach to the things we want to bring into our days means just that—to treat them as an artist would treat a practice, without harsh consequences for 'failure'.

Instead of attaching punishments to what we set out to do, we can nurture what I now call 'delightful discipline'—that which is driven by a curiosity for knowledge, a commitment to the practice, without the rigid sense of obedience or punishing rules that can stifle us. The focus is on training and the pursuit of knowledge, which can subsequently bring flow, focus and enjoyment to the things we wish to do.

Delightful discipline is by nature flexible, and therefore more compatible with our human tendency to wobble. Punishing discipline tends to ignore that our desires can change, whereas delightful discipline can help us become more attuned to them— sometimes we want to read instead of write, and both can contribute to our knowledge and skill.

Instead of over-indexing on adhering to rules, delightful discipline can take a 'most days' approach, where we commit to the practice or skill over the long haul, stay attuned to our energy levels and remember to start again tomorrow if we need to.

Delightful discipline can be both the impetus and what sustains us when it comes to doing the thing. If we start with fascination or an interest in something, we may well encounter flow and find momentum.

Ways to be delightfully disciplined

- What if we were disciplined about kindness?

- What if we were disciplined about loving the problem?

- What if we were disciplined about what we look for?

- What if we were disciplined about what nourished us?

- What if we were disciplined about how we talk to ourselves?

- What if we were disciplined about who we let in?

- What if we were disciplined about reserving judgement?

- What if we were disciplined about allowing for space?

- What if we were disciplined about listening?

- What if we were disciplined about giving compliments?

- What if we were disciplined about letting go of things not meant for us?

- What if we were disciplined about how we treat special things?

- What if we were disciplined about saying 'I don't know'?

- What if we were disciplined about doing things differently?

- What if we were disciplined about pausing to think?

- What if we were disciplined about finding our own way?

Swap dread for delight

What I've observed is that we don't need more rules or more self-discipline to get things done—we need to make things more delightful so that we actually enjoy doing them. It's simple, really: we keep doing the things we find enjoyable, meaning we keep practising, which is at the heart of discipline.

Instead of starting out in a way that will soon exhaust us, we sustain our energy by going slow and steady, sprinkling delight along the way. This is how we can find momentum in delight. To have fun—to cultivate delight in what we do—we often have to be driven by what behavioural psychologists call *intrinsic motivation*. That's the act of doing something without any obvious external rewards—or doing something because it's inherently enjoyable and interesting to us. By contrast, *extrinsic motivation* refers to what others want us to do—and by effect often feels punishing.

Sometimes we can put these things off because we're waiting to find the motivation—however motivation isn't something we find, but rather something we cultivate. This is known as the 'motivation trap': despite the common belief, motivation does not precede action; action precedes motivation.

So what precedes action? I think that's fascination—we are more likely to take action if we are interested in something, so we must first find the thing that interests us. Often this comes naturally: we might find ourselves fascinated by cooking, writing, learning something new. But we can also seek pleasure in such activities. I've found that when I swap punishment for delight, I take action. For example, my previous attempts at exercising focused on dread, as they were tied to a measurable outcome: to change a number on a scale. When I looked for delight in exercise—to feel good, rather than to look good—it became more appealing to go for a run. The reward was in the doing itself, rather than in the outcome. Because it was now inherently enjoyable, I exercised more often, inadvertently building a regular practice (or discipline) of running—and gradually I reached my goal of running for five kilometres, and later ten.

Now when I'm stuck, I try to find a way to start with delight rather than dread. Starting with fascination or delight is far more appealing than being bored or frustrated with a regular practice before you've even begun. It's also more sustainable, because you're less likely to give up in the way you might when a practice is attached to punishment. As the writer and activist Carly Findlay told me, 'I don't want to push myself so much that I don't enjoy it.' We have a better chance of doing something if we enjoy doing it—if we find it too difficult or unenjoyable, it doesn't matter how much willpower we have, we probably won't keep at it for very long.

Not only are we more likely to find momentum and keep doing something if we enjoy it, but we also need to protect the enjoyment or delight we find as we progress. To do this, we can make use of the 'Zeigarnik effect'. This psychological phenomenon explains our tendency to keep thinking about the things we have left incomplete, whether it's ticking off a to-do item, reaching inbox zero or eating the last Oreo. Not finishing a task creates mental tension, which keeps it at the forefront of our memory. Because we like closure, the only thing that will relieve this tension is completing the task. But there is one very important caveat to this: the tasks have to be attractive and possible in order for this phenomenon to take effect. If we find the task too difficult, the Zeigarnik effect does not occur, and instead we can find ourselves overwhelmed or anxious.

Delight may be at centre of the Venn diagram of what we find attractive and possible—and we can find ways to create this delightful tension for ourselves. Defining an end point sometimes means holding yourself back when you still have gas in the tank, but learning when to stop can help us sustain ourselves over time. As Ernest Hemingway wrote in *A Moveable Feast*, 'I always worked until I had something done, and I always stopped when I knew what was going to happen next. That way I could be sure of going on the next day.' While this example is specific to the writing process, I've applied it to running, to life admin tasks, to almost anything—stop while the going is good, so you'll be sure to keep going when you recommence because you've made it attractive and possible to do so.

So to continue doing something, it's important to remember to put joy ahead of duty. Too often we have it the other way around—other people's demands of us come before our own, work is prioritised over rest, and we fixate on the result rather than the process. Even when we encounter something we enjoy, we can be quick to fasten it to a punishing schedule: we should run six mornings a week, we should read five books on vacation, we should turn our hobby of pickling into a side hustle. Where did all the joy go? It disappears amid the regulations we set up and our focus on the outcome.

Starting with delight is about finding what intrinsically motivates us, instead of being derailed by extrinsic measures. Maybe we can do this with our lives, too. Rather than think we have to endure something to get to something else, what if we did more of what we want right now? This is an attitude I've often noticed in the creative people I've interviewed—starting out, they put the work they want to be doing into the world, and eventually they find that people will commission that type of work from them. When they couldn't find the job they wanted, they created it. To get what we want, we often need to start by doing it—not to wait for the opportunity to arise, but rather to create it ourselves.

Again, the hardest part of the equation here is starting. So we must remember to make what we want to do attractive and possible. In other words, we need to make it as easy as possible to begin. It can take a long time to get started, even with something we've had success with starting before—each day I want to go for a run, I still sense some resistance in myself, because motivation can ebb and flow. But I remind myself that starting is the hardest part, and I have a better chance of succeeding if I make it delightful. Perhaps I can make it enjoyable by running with a friend, or make it easier by putting my running shoes out the night before. We don't need to add another layer of dread to things by setting up rules and milestones. We can simply make a start.

Encountering delight in the discomfort

'Delightful discipline' doesn't mean everything is immediately enjoyable, but rather that we can shape the things we wish to do in such a way that we can encounter delight.

Naturally, there will be things we have to do that we don't want to do. Even in such instances, I believe they can be driven by delightful discipline. That's because delightful discipline acknowledges that sometimes it is the very presence of a challenge, resistance or difficulty that makes the process of doing something more inherently worthwhile.

Delight can be both the driver and the by-product of practising a skill. That is, something can be rendered delightful through the process of doing it. When we practise a skill, we can encounter 'flow'—a term coined by the psychologist Mihaly Csikszentmihalyi to mean an act of deep concentration that brings feelings of clarity, effortlessness and enjoyment. We enter a state of flow when certain conditions are met: when the action and our awareness merge; where we have no fear of failure; when our self-consciousness disappears; when our sense of time becomes distorted; and when the activity becomes autotelic, or an end in itself.

When we are in flow, time tends to pass by quickly. Perhaps delightful discipline is one way we take advantage of the holiday paradox we met earlier—how time seems to pass more quickly when we are doing something fun, but after the moment passes it feels longer. A challenge is often novel; a new experience can be what makes something a challenge as we've never done it before. So we can alter our perceptions of time by keeping our brain active, continually learning skills and ideas, and exploring new places—even if it's difficult at the time, we can look back at it with delight.

To be in a state of flow, there has to be some element of challenge and focus—of immersing ourselves in something that requires perseverance. Such experiences are often associated with playing music, viewing or making art, or engaging in physical activity or sport. But it's not just about our work or creative pursuits—we can cultivate the flow of delightful discipline in how we approach any manner of ordinary experiences in our daily lives: making something instead of buying it, repairing your own bicycle, solving a puzzle.

The hurdle, however, may be that we often favour convenience over experience. Sometimes we're not ready yet; sometimes we take the easy option. In many ways, our modern lives have been designed that way—our consumerist society sees us working more to build the life we are told to desire (even if, in some cases, we are denied access to it), leaving us time-poor, with convenience the only option. But perhaps we're attracted to the quick and seemingly effortless also because it's easier to distract ourselves than it is to immerse ourselves.

We think we want comfort or convenience, when actually it's discomfort and challenge that are necessary and fulfilling. Life isn't friction-free for the vast majority of us.

If you have the means, you can order in good food, get rideshare whenever you need it, orchestrate a convenient life in which friction is reduced—but your engagement is dulled. Perhaps this is one reason people enjoy playing records—the act of getting up, flipping the disc over and placing the needle back down is a small, delightful challenge that makes the experience more engaging. Small inconveniences always bring me back into the moment— when I'm waiting for a pizza to arrive, for example, I'm able to disappear into the vortex of my devices, whereas if I'm making my own meal, I'm immersed in a task where I can find flow. We can so quickly forget that inconvenience, challenge and tension can bring more satisfaction than ease.

Sometimes, what looks like the more effortful or punishing option is actually more satisfying—more delightful—because it requires that we engage with a challenge. In *This One Wild and Precious Life*, the writer and activist Sarah Wilson made a case for riding a bike or running places instead of taking a car. As she pointed out, it might seem like more effort to ride somewhere, but it's actually a lot easier than driving to a gym, finding a carpark, hopping on a stationary bike, driving back home and then commuting to work. As Wilson put it, 'Why not just ride to work and be done with it in a quarter of the time?'

Riding a bike to work might not be a possibility for all of us, but perhaps inspecting where we are choosing comfort over challenge can be. A starting point might be to look at what is a 'punishing' discipline—say, driving to the gym—and considering whether there's a more delightful option—say, walking to work instead. Alternatively, we can look at what we are outsourcing and see if there's a way that doing it ourselves would bring more engagement. We may, through pursuing the seemingly inconvenient choice, even experience a sense of delight.

The inconvenience is often where we find flow and solve problems for ourselves. When I interviewed the author Annie Raser-Rowland, she explained that we build confidence from these small acts of self-reliance. She spoke about how being resourceful in our everyday life can give us ample opportunity to experience flow and become engrossed in our creative and physical abilities. We might learn to repair or repurpose items we'd otherwise dispose of, which not only teaches us a new skill but may also increase our appreciation of the item we can continue using. The more we practise resourcefulness in this way, the more we can expand our capacity for delight.

Flow isn't simply something we can stumble into with ease—such moments are not passive or relaxing, but rather stem from a dedication to pursuing a challenge. As Mihaly Csikszentmihalyi put it, 'The best moments usually occur when a person's body or mind is stretched to its limits in a voluntary effort to accomplish something difficult and worthwhile. Optimal experience is thus something that we make happen.' This sometimes means we have to face the blank page, or do something dull and repetitive along the path to finding flow, and see the boredom or tedium that can come with it as part of the challenge. Again, to stick at something, we need to find some semblance of enjoyment or pleasure, rather than see it as a chore. But we can render the mundanity of repetition into something delightful, too. Perhaps the antidote to fleeing from the things we want to do, the things that feel uncomfortable, is to bring an element of delight into the discipline. We can pay attention to how much we enjoy hard work when we are immersed in it, and delight in the challenges of the day.

Perhaps that's the very appeal of ritual or having a creative practice. For the artist Rachel Burke, the doing of something, over and over, is what allows her to discover something new. Known for her quirky art projects—such as creating pompoms with attached apologies, or attaching jewels to cans she's found in the pantry—she told me staying with something through repetition brings beauty.

'It might start as one thing, but if I look from the beginning to the end of the project, it will have changed and that only came about through repetition. I guess that's why I really love doing these little series and things.'

We have to show up again and again, even when we don't feel inspired or other things seem more appealing, in order to discover something new. As the author and artist Lisa Congdon told me, 'It's actually in the monotony that the magic happens, but you just don't know it when you're going through it.'

The creative process has this reality built in: there will be times that we resist doing it, or want to quit, but often it's at those moments when it feels monotonous or like it's not working that we are on the precipice of something new. As Congdon added, nothing is delightful all the way through. 'By a certain point, it feels like drudgery. But underneath the lack of new ideas or the uncertainty of what direction to take something in is fear—if you can push through that fear and force yourself to sit down and do the thing, that is where the growth happens.' We must keep our bum on the proverbial seat in order to encounter something delightful once more. In *Why We Write*, the author Isabel Allende was quoted: 'Show up, show up, show up, and after a while the muse shows up, too. If she doesn't show up invited, eventually she just shows up.' Delightful discipline can be similar—motivation or interest may wax and wane, but if we keep coming back to it, there is bound to be something we encounter as a result. Delightful discipline is not a hack or a short cut—it's an invitation, a practice in asking ourselves what will introduce more presence and joy into our days, and following that.

Beginning the day with delight

If starting is the hardest part of any new discipline, and we can help ourselves by making it more inherently pleasurable to begin, then perhaps we can apply this logic to our days as well.

Popular productivity theory suggests that we should get the unenjoyable stuff out of the way first to ensure a better day. For example, the 'Eat the Frog' method popularised by author Brian Tracy suggests we tackle our most dreaded task or challenging agenda item first thing in the morning, when we're less susceptible to distraction. Maybe it's exercise, or a difficult project at work. By doing the dreaded thing first, we'll feel better about the rest of our day.

Starting your day with the most challenging task has its perks—we'll no longer be haunted by the dreaded task, or feel as susceptible to the 'if only' spiral. Yet beginning our day with our most dreaded task still tethers our days to productivity—which ignores the many ways we can open a day. The poet David Whyte expressed this sentiment well in a Facebook post by TED: 'That moment of waking is an incredible opportunity, and it's quite a tragedy if you go straight to your to-do list.'

Perhaps there's something to be said for waking and beginning our day with delight rather than dread. When I interviewed the farmer and chef Matthew Evans, he described how he has recently been starting his day with porridge and a dollop of homemade clotted cream, because he prefers to begin, not end, the day with a highlight. 'Putting a dab of that on my porridge in the morning with brown sugar? Delightful. It's so early in the day, you think that the day can't get better than that. Most days it does, but it's still pretty wonderful.'

Inspired by Evans, this is what I've come to think of as the 'Eat the Clotted Cream' method: if we start our day with the most delightful thing, it might have a ripple effect on our mood as the day unfolds—if we begin by feeling the day can't get any better than this, we'll likely bring a mood that proves it can. Personally, I find it easier to do things I don't want to do when I'm in a good mood, and the metaphorical clotted cream might be the sweetener I need.

Besides, we might not be hardwired for reward—making our efforts to delay gratification superfluous. While common wisdom suggests that we will put in a level of effort that matches the reward we expect, a 2020 study from researchers at Queen Mary University of London, published in the journal *Behavioural Brain Research*, found that high rewards are not enough for us to put in the effort.

Dr Agata Ludwiczak, a research fellow at Queen Mary University of London and lead author of the study, explained: 'We have found that there isn't a direct relationship between the amount of reward that is at stake and the amount of effort people actually put in. This is because when we make choices about what effort to put in, we are motivated by the rewards we expect to get back. But at the point at which we come to actually do what we had said we would do, we focus on the level of effort we have to actually put in rather than the rewards we hoped we would get.'

In other words, we may realise the effort is too much and give up. For example, getting up early to 'eat the frog' might seem like a wise choice, but when the alarm sounds it's not necessarily going to motivate us to get out of bed, because the reward suddenly isn't as appealing. But if something delightful is waiting for us, it may be the very thing to coax us out.

Naturally, that delightful something doesn't have to be literal clotted cream—just as you don't have to eat a literal frog. What I particularly like about this analogy is that it's about savouring the variety of flavours and textures we encounter in a day—rather than forcing ourselves to swallow a particularly gruesome one.

The beautiful thing about delight is that it comes in many flavours. For inspiration, we can turn to what delighted us as kids and start our day with that—it might be writing, a meandering walk, painting or even playing dress-ups. The craft-based designer Kitiya Palaskas makes a game out of getting dressed in the morning, adding a limitation: she can't wear the same thing twice in a week. This turns an ordinary activity into a creative act. As she told me, 'I feel like if you just wake up in the morning and go straight to work, it can be such a bummer, so I like to treat myself a bit each day so life doesn't feel like a chore.'

Delight might also be about setting a mood. What's the thing you most enjoy about each day? What's the very thing you wish you could find time for? Start the day with that—and observe how the day and your mood unfolds from there.

Starting your day early to have a solitary hour might be your way of finding delight. Or perhaps it's answering emails in bed to ease yourself into the day. Personally, I find putting the dishes away first thing in the morning to be rather delightful—a clearing of yesterday, a beginning of today. It's about whatever delights you, even if it sounds counterintuitive to others.

And given it's about finding what works for you, maybe you'd prefer the delayed gratification of ending your day with delight. Whether we start or end our day with delight may depend on what's happening in our lives—maybe you want to get straight into a hot bath after you get back from work as a way to soothe after a busy day; maybe you want to stop by a bookstore during your lunch hour; maybe you take ten minutes to meditate in the car after dropping off the kids, or listen to your favourite podcast. Whatever our circumstance, we can scatter delight through our days.

Another option is to commence the week with delight. When the artist Ken Done made the transition between working in advertising and being a full-time painter, he wanted to start each week by doing the work he was most passionate about, so he reserved Mondays for painting. Another anecdote I'll always remember from my conversation with Ken concerned a gnome figurine he kept in his studio that would make a farting noise when he left for the day—a delightful reminder not to take ourselves too seriously or congratulate ourselves too much. We must begin again tomorrow, after all.

So whether it's something simple, delicious, easeful, playful or passionate, we can experiment with rendering something more delightful. What delights us will change, and therefore what creates momentum in our day will change too. Sometimes the periodic abandonment of the delightful discipline can be the very thing that reminds us of why something delighted us in the first place, or alert us to something anew. The important thing is to be alive to the flavours of the day, rather than dread the day.

13

The Push and Pull
of Distraction

We have to try to cure our faults by attention and not by will.
Simone Weil, *Gravity and Grace*

Sometimes a day can disappear in a distracted haze. We're pulled by the news, by other people, by the thing over there. We are also pulled internally by our thoughts, feelings, urges and compulsions. We ruminate, we obsess about an ex, we remember that bill we didn't pay or that awkward thing we said three years ago. We follow various threads of distraction—the exciting, the interesting, the easier, the numbing—weaving between thoughts and tasks in our days, making messy, unfinished tapestries of what we were once focused on.

Such distractions can hijack our plans for the day. A feeling can easily fling us from doing the thing, and we either become distracted by the inner turmoil or look for ways to pacify our restlessness. Often it's our doubts, our fears, our boredoms, our regrets, our guilt that pushes us towards external distractions—our phones, our email, our unopened tabs, our sudden desire to see what our high-school nemesis is up to now. It's far easier to scroll through endless reels than it is to sit with our own boredom, loneliness, anxiety or dread.

While the pull of distraction has become synonymous with our devices, we have long been susceptible to it. The University of California, San Francisco, professor Adam Gazzaley observed that all of our interactions with the world are the outcome of an ongoing competition between bottom-up and top-down forces. Top-down forces stem from how our own goals influence our behaviour, and allow us to direct our attention to what's important and filter out what isn't. As Gazzaley wrote in 'Taking Control of Your Distracted Mind' for *Thrive Global*, 'Top-down has broken the reflexive perception-action cycle that drives the behaviours of other animals; it has freed us from being slaves to our sensory world, and has thus fostered the conditions necessary for the emergence of culture, art, music, language, and technology.'

Bottom-up forces, on the other hand, stem from unexpected events and novel occurrences that command our attention. While reflexive responses to distractions or interruptions are crucial for our survival—say, bursts of light, sounds, vibrations and the call of our name—we can see how our devices cleverly mimic these mechanisms: the vibrating, the dinging, the brightening screens, the constant use of our name in push notifications.

Such features, coupled with unprecedented access to information and the increase in multitasking, have shifted the balance of power. Not only is there more noise, but we are also more sensitive to bottom-up distraction in our daily lives—we're more distractable and less able to direct our attention towards what matters most.

Not only are we pushed and pulled to external distractions, but those distractions are also changing us. What the Netflix documentary *The Social Dilemma* made clear is that when we're not paying for the product, we are the product—in the case of social-media platforms, our attention is being sold to advertisers. But it goes deeper than that; as the computer scientist Jaron Lanier said, 'It's the gradual, slight, imperceptible change in your own behaviour and perception that is the product.'

Our human desire for connection is contorted in the digital world, and as a result it is contorting us. The instant gratification of sharing something online, the rapid news cycle and the constant churn of information we're exposed to are dampening our tolerance of quietness, boredom and empty time. We are changing in perceptible and imperceptible ways.

In her TED Talk 'Connected, But Alone?', the psychologist Sherry Turkle explained how our devices are changing our minds and hearts because they offer us three gratifying fantasies: that we can put our attention wherever we want it to be; that we will always be heard; and that we will never have to be alone. It's this third idea—that we will never have to be alone—that is central to changing our psyches, said Turkle. 'Because the moment that people are alone, even for a few seconds, they become anxious, they panic, they fidget, they reach for a device. Just think of people at a checkout line or at a red light. Being alone feels like a problem that needs to be solved. And so people try to solve it by connecting. But here, connection is more like a symptom than a cure.'

Constant connection is changing how we think and behave. We spend an evening on social media instead of going out with friends, we check Instagram rather than engage with the person in front of us, we scroll Tinder while our date is in the bathroom— and wind up feeling more isolated. This never-ending stream of high-tech advances has challenged our brains at a fundamental level, negatively impacting our work, study, stress levels, anxiety, relationships, health and sleep. Our obsession can cause distraction, our bingeing can cause a negative spiral in our wellbeing, and our fear of missing out spoils what we experience in our own lives.

Even when we recognise such harms and try to wean ourselves off our devices, the pull can feel impossible to resist. The issue may be that many of these distractions have been designed to trigger an immediate feel-good effect, which in the moment feels more pleasurable than whatever we are distracting ourselves from. But that feel-good effect quickly wears off, and so we keep returning for more, increasingly losing control over time. As Associate Professor Peggy Kern from the University of Melbourne's Centre for Wellbeing Science explains, 'We may think we are in control of our social-media usage, but in fact it is controlling us, which only becomes apparent when you try to change your behaviour, but cannot. These can be the roots of addiction, which become increasingly harder to escape over time, reinforced by the very design of the technology itself.'

A common solution is to eliminate distractions—but how plausible is that when even those who have designed such addictive features have a hard time resisting them?

I DIDN'T DO THE THING TODAY

Perhaps it's less about trying to rid our days of inevitable distractions, and more about shaping how they can lead us back to ourselves and each other. According to Turkle, 'Our fantasies of substitution have cost us. Now we all need to focus on the many, many ways technology can lead us back to our real lives, our own bodies, our own communities, our own politics, our own planet. They need us.'

Instead of constant connection, we need to practise the art of connection—and we can do this through cultivating attention.

Stretching our attention

Before we cultivate attention, we have to acknowledge the rare commodity that it is. We live in an attention economy: entertainment platforms, advertisers and media outlets use our attention as currency, and it goes to the highest bidder. On top of this exchange, the various parts of our daily lives also compete for our attention—the emails we answer, the errands we run, the call to a friend. All of this is a transaction, as Charlie Warzel wrote in 'I Talked to the Cassandra of the Internet Age' for *The New York Times*: 'When you pay attention to one thing, you ignore something else.'

Amid this constant exchange of attention, it feels rare that we give or receive it fully. Perhaps in the constant push and pull of our attention, we've lost touch with how to lend it. Recalling a first date, a friend told me about the most romantic gesture she had encountered in recent times: as she sat down with this relative stranger, he reached for his phone, brought it to the centre of the table and switched it off in plain view, before returning it to his pocket. He was signifying that his attention was all hers.

As Simone Weil wrote in *Gravity and Grace*, 'Attention is the rarest and purest form of generosity.' We see this in the very etymology of the word 'attention', which comes from the Latin verb *attendere*, meaning 'to stretch towards' something. So to give someone or something our full attention is to extend ourselves, our resources, our energy, our generosity.

The gift of attention can be extended to other parts of our lives. It can be given societally, to pressing problems such as income inequality, the climate crisis and systemic racial injustice. Directing our attention to such issues is signalling what we value, and how we will spend our resources.

To extend ourselves in this way and pay attention is essential to drive change, but it's likely not something we are capable of maintaining ceaselessly. If we paid constant attention or overstretched ourselves, we'd no doubt find ourselves snapping back like an elastic band.

Our modern world often stretches our attention. The 24-hour news cycle is one example. The journalist Oliver Burkeman has observed in himself and others a tendency to live inside the news—people are shifting their psychological centre of gravity to the news cycle to the point that it somehow becomes more real to them than the concrete world of their own work, family and friends, and the drama of their daily lives.

Of course, local and global events do impact our daily lives and deserve our attention. Not only do we each experience varying personal challenges and societal injustices first-hand, but paying attention to the injustices in the world outside our own can be the precursor to change and action. But is 'living inside the news' really paying attention, or are we simply distracted by the opinions, circumstances and lives of others? Stretching our attention to a point that's unsustainable can sometimes be the very thing that lulls us into inaction—if we are up to date with the news, that can feel like action enough, and we needn't do anything about it. Conversely, we feel steeped in our own powerlessness as we continue to refresh our screens, becoming further stifled. In both instances, we may be paying constant attention, but we are missing the part where we act or connect generously.

It may be that constant attention dulls our attention. It's rather amusing to read the words of author Sarah Chauncey Woolsey in a preface to a collection of letters by Jane Austen from 1892: 'Our modern times, when steam and electricity have linked together the ends of the earth, and the very air seems teeming with news, agitations, discussions. We have barely time to recover our breath between post and post; and the morning paper with its statements of disaster and its hints of still greater evils to be, is scarcely outlived, when, lo! in comes the evening issue, contradicting the news of the morning, to be sure, but full of omens and auguries of its own to stew our pillows with the seed of wakefulness.' What would she make of a 24-hour news cycle!

Our nerves may well be in a state of unwholesome disrepair, not only from the constant bombardment of contradicting and polarising news, but also from an endless stream of updates from friends, foes and strangers. We blame ourselves for not keeping up, but perhaps we're just not meant to be aware of what thousands of people think.

We're not designed to listen all the time, to pay attention all the time, to be constantly connected, or to extend and stretch all the time. Perhaps we need to recognise how to distribute our attention in ways that can be sustainable for ourselves and generous to others. According to Burkeman, 'To stay sane, you need at least one foot planted firmly in your world: the world of your job and neighbourhood, that letter you need to mail, the pasta you're cooking for dinner, the novel you're reading with your book group, and that guy on your street who never cleans up after his dog—the world where you can have an effect, even if I've admittedly yet to have one with the dog guy.'

So how do we keep one foot planted firmly in our own days? How do we find that balance between paying attention and protecting ourselves from overextension? Perhaps we should start by analysing how we spend this limited resource that is our attention. Instead of digesting everything we see, hear or read, we can be more discerning in what we offer the generosity of our attention to.

Paying attention to what you pay attention to

What if we measured our days not by how many minutes flitted by in distraction, but by what we pay attention to—what we hear, what we see, who we connect with, what we learn? As the writer Amy Krouse Rosenthal put it in a tweet, 'To anyone trying to figure out their life, pay attention to what you pay attention to. That's pretty much all the information you need.'

Our experiences account for so much more than what we witness through a screen, but if many of us paid attention to what we paid attention to each day, what would we make of our life? Would we like what we see, who we are? Maybe we wouldn't enjoy being a person who checks their phone first thing in the morning, cradles their device at night, or scrolls dating apps at parties instead of noticing that cute stranger by the snack table.

But even when we become aware of how our devices are ruling us, we struggle to rein in our usage. We promise ourselves we won't take the phone to bed tonight, only for it to creep back in when the lights go out. Willpower alone won't curb our addiction. Instead, it is attention that can serve as an antidote to distraction: once we notice what pinches our attention in our days, we can begin to shape our experiences, our perceptions, and thus who we are.

This is how attention and distraction are interlinked—we can distract ourselves by putting our attention towards something else: for example, focusing on finding the perfect writing desk instead of writing. This kind of attention—on the perfect environment, the ideal body, our measure of success or something else—can be distractions in disguise. Attention misdirected can rob us of what we need to apply to other things that we really want to do. This brings us back to the importance of paying attention to what we pay attention to, so we can make a choice about whether we want to keep directing our attention towards what has distracted us.

Distraction dissipates when we notice it, because noticing it leads to attention, and attention can lead to focus. Despite the cunning design of our distractions, we retain the capacity to choose what we attend to. We can choose what we do with this hour, who we listen to, who we ignore, who we amplify, what habits and hobbies we cultivate, what opportunities we take. It is this reclaiming of our choice in what we pay attention to that reconnects us with ourselves and our sense of agency.

When we pay attention to what we pay attention to, we can notice and discover what we love. As the teacher, Sister Sarah Joan, tells her student, Christine 'Lady Bird' McPherson, in the film *Lady Bird*, 'Don't you think maybe they are the same thing? Love and attention?' If paying attention and love are the same thing, then we can ask ourselves moment to moment if we are spending our love on the important and fulfilling things.

Not only can we notice what we love when we pay attention, but love can also bloom in the attention we give something. Paying attention enough for love to bloom in this way cannot be hurried—we must allow ourselves to linger in the moment instead of rushing to the next, to take in the details, to engage with something by stretching towards it. We can easily miss opportunities for love—that is, for cultivating a great interest and pleasure in something—because we overlook the moment.

This tendency to rush might speak to our busy lives, but also signifies how awkward we sometimes feel in a spare moment: how we have been taught to rush, and how difficult it can be to do nothing but notice. I'll always remember the anecdote I heard from curator Lesley Harding about the charismatic artist Mirka Mora. After a visit to her studio, Lesley would always offer to clean up the cups and plates of leftover cakes, but Mora would always decline and say, '*Non, ma chérie*, I just want to sit with them for a while and think about our conversation.'

To broaden our capacity for love, we must broaden what we pay attention to—and to broaden what we pay attention to, we must broaden the moment. We must sit with the dishes in the sink for a moment longer, and generously extend an ear back to the conversations we've just had. Lingering broadens the moment by encouraging us to take our time. If we give space to spare time, we allow more life to happen naturally, and for something like love to bubble up. This is how love blooms—once it reveals itself to us, it leads us to more we can love, more we can notice and pay attention to.

But, of course, this isn't to ignore that love itself is complicated. Sometimes we love the very thing that interrupts us—a member of our family, a demanding project, a new pet. We can also encounter unrequited love in the things we pay attention to—not everything we stretch towards will stretch back. Attention misdirected can be misery, but it can also be the making of us; to quote a line from the film *Adaptation*, 'You are what you love, not what loves you.'

Perhaps this sentiment excludes what pretends to love us, in the form of the hearts and likes we see on a screen. When we log on to social media to see what's waiting for us, we receive attention back for giving our attention to the platform and the advertisers that want it. This is an illusory form of attention that often distracts us from the fact that our attention is being sold.

So how do we direct our attention—or spend our love—in ways that feel reciprocal or fulfilling, and manage even those distractions we love? I rather like the idea of setting aside an 'attention hour'—a designated pocket of time devoted to paying attention to what we have been paying attention to. You can tuck yourself away in a quiet, distraction-free space with just a pen and paper, and ponder what you've been reading, learning, thinking about, giving your attention to—or perhaps your desires, your relationships, the passions you have been neglecting.

The scholar Joseph Campbell described something like this in *The Power of Myth*: 'You must have a room, or a certain hour or so a day, where you don't know what was in the newspapers that morning, you don't know who your friends are, you don't know what you owe anybody, you don't know what anybody owes to you. This is a place where you can simply experience and bring forth what you are and what you might be. This is the place of creative incubation. At first you may find that nothing happens there. But if you have a sacred place and use it, something eventually will happen.'

We rarely afford ourselves this luxury of reflection, but it might have more importance than we give it credit for. As the French philosopher Blaise Pascal wrote in *Pensées*, 'All of humanity's problems stem from man's inability to sit quietly in a room alone.' It's during this time alone, as we pay attention to what we've been paying attention to, that we might find the solution, think of the right thing to say, or identify what has been pushing us towards soothing distractions in the first instance.

Another form of being intentional with our attention is the deep work approach, popularised by Cal Newport, mentioned earlier. A way to focus without distraction on a cognitively demanding task, deep work may appear to be about managing your calendar and blocking out time, but it's just as much about attention. The two may be interlinked: time and attention are our two most precious resources, and both happen to be how we spend our love.

Indeed, what is time unless we pay attention to its passing? Maybe paying attention is more meaningful to our lives than being productive or managing our time—to paraphrase the poet William

Meredith, the worst that can be said of a person is that they did not pay attention. The ability to pay attention to what we pay attention to, to relish time spent in a room alone, to stretch our attention to others generously—no, perhaps this is not just where love blooms, but where we find its very meaning.

A method for cultivating attention

We are surrounded by distractions, and we carry them within ourselves too, so rather than searching for the hack that will eliminate them, we might be better off cobbling together various methods for cultivating attention and applying them as we see fit. Here are some that have worked for me.

Know what breaks your attention

Perhaps it's not about squeezing more into our days, but removing what breaks our attention. Whether it's meetings, laundry lists or social media, we can scatter seemingly harmless interruptions in our day that take longer to recuperate from than we might anticipate. We might schedule a coffee meeting that's only half an hour in our calendar, for example, but we forget the bumpers of time surrounding it (a commute to the cafe and back), and the break in our attention beforehand caused by the knowledge that we have somewhere to be. As Charles Dickens once said when rejecting an invitation, 'The mere consciousness of an engagement will sometimes worry a whole day.'

The illustrator Maira Kalman told me that she doesn't like to have lunch meetings because it often breaks the momentum of her day—so she'll often meet someone for breakfast instead, and then everyone can go on their merry way. Maybe other people are less of a peril for you, but the lesson remains: know what breaks your attention so you can send it on its merry way.

Attend to one thing at a time
Managing our attention is really about managing the moment—and in a single moment, we can only really attend to one thing. Resist the urge to toggle, to multitask, to flit between things; instead, focus on one task, one browser tab, one moment at a time.

Attending to one thing at a time is also a practice in taking on less—setting the bar lower and picking just one small thing to attend to in the moment. Often we think we can achieve much more in a given timeframe than is possible.

Protect your attention
Popular advice suggests turning off notifications and deleting any time-wasting apps from your devices. I've lost count of the times I've deleted apps on my phone, only to hours later download them again. I've installed app blockers and set time limits, only to then delete the app blocker so I can access the app again. I've turned off notifications, only to compulsively check Tinder and WhatsApp for messages that may have come through.

Again, attention is the only antidote to distraction: instead of eliminating distractions, focus on protecting your attention. A common suggestion is to schedule focused time where we put a shield around our attention. For me, this means working in 45-minute blocks—during these blocks, I put my phone away, block distracting websites in my browser, and sit at my desk.

Most importantly, perhaps, is the little desk bell I ding to signal the beginning of the first session. It might seem trivial or even a bit silly, but over time this simple habit has become a subtle sound cue for me that it's time to pay attention.

Sustain your attention through regular breaks

For this multi-prong approach to take hold, we need to take mental breaks in order to sustain our attention. The break can often be the reward: instead of being perpetually interrupted by breaks in our attention, we can hold our attention in the knowledge that a break will soon come.

Not all breaks are created equal, either. Studies suggest a short burst of exercise, going outside, daydreaming, taking a nap or talking to someone on the phone are restorative breaks. In my 45-minute focus sessions, I listen to the same song, 'Ambient Chopin' by Peter M. Murray. It's 22 minutes and 59 seconds long, so when I hear the short space of silence before it repeats, I know I'm halfway through and it's time for a short '20-20-20' eye break: every twenty minutes, I focus on an object twenty feet away for twenty seconds.

Cultivate attention through your senses

When we don't have a clear distinction between the different environments we occupy—say, when we work from home—our habits usually associated with these different parts of our lives can become blurred. Luckily, we can shape our environments in small ways to help us ease into a certain task.

According to the theory of writer and designer Jack Cheng, every object, room and environment we interact with emits a 'habit field', which is a collection of associations that influence our behaviour. 'First, define how you want to split your activities across various tools or spaces,' Cheng recommended, 'and then commit to keeping activities separate to fortify respective habit fields. Every time you sit down, try to ask yourself, "How are my actions going to affect the habit fields of the objects around me?"'

We can create a new habit field and reinforce it through repetition. For example, the author and artist Austin Kleon keeps two desks: a tidy digital desk for focused writing, and a messy analogue desk for creating his artworks. We can set up various habit fields to both cultivate focus and embrace distraction. For example, sit in the same chair every time you want to do focused work, and choose a 'distraction chair' for when you need a break.

If we can't make adjustments to our physical environment, we can make use of our senses. So light a candle for scent, make a cup of tea for taste, listen to a playlist for sound, put on a comfy pair of socks as a physical marker that you're stepping into the zone, or close your office door to signal the end of the workday.

Allow for distractions

Some days, the methods we practise to cultivate attention feel futile. Given that we face countless interruptions in a day, perhaps there is a way to work with them. I remember speaking with the permaculture educator Kirsten Bradley about how some days simply go awry on her farm. 'If the goats get out, then all bets are off,' she said, 'and you have to run off and chase the goat down the gully!' We needn't judge how the day unfolds. Some days we succeed in staying focused on the task at hand, some days we're distracted by other chores, and some days the goat gets out.

Following the thread of distraction can sometimes be what helps get us unstuck—especially if we turn to something physical. This is Bradley's trusted approach. 'If we get stuck, we can go plant leeks or something. When you get it right, it's a really great balance between deep thinking work and work that utilises your entire body to solve a problem.'

If you can't find focus, step into a distraction you enjoy, rather than being stuck in aimless and ceaseless distraction. Go out wandering on a sunny afternoon, make endless cups of tea, fold laundry when you're meant to be working, binge-watch a show, cook something, listen to a podcast, answer emails, rearrange the bathroom cabinet, watch the windowpane on rainy nights. Be fully present with the thing you are doing, rather than feeling guilty about the thing you're not doing.

Succumbing to distractions can make our days feel chaotic— what we were meant to be doing now needs to be squeezed in with all the things we have to do tomorrow. But despite the snowball of tasks this can create, distraction happens to us all. Perhaps we simply need to account for it more—or even embrace it. There are times when distraction can be a reprieve, or even help alert us to something that needs our attention. As the Argentine author Julio Cortázar wrote in *Around the Day in Eighty Worlds*, 'All profound distraction opens certain doors. You have to allow yourself to be distracted when you are unable to concentrate.'

Maybe there's beauty in our messy tapestries of distraction after all. Berating ourselves for letting our minds wander or for doing something other than what we're supposed to be doing only sends us further down the spiral. So why not sometimes follow the distraction, open new doors, enjoy chasing the proverbial goat around the yard? Perhaps it's better to weave with what we have, and be okay with a few loose threads.

14

The Trying Pursuit of Perfection

Nothing is perfect. There are lumps in it.
James Stephens, *The Crock of Gold*

Perfectionism tells us that in order to make progress, what we do must be perfect. We see this across our daily lives—in how we approach our routines, our creative projects, our work, our relationships, our appearance, our parenting, as well as social justice and environmental issues. Yet our fixation on being perfect can prevent us from making any progress at all.

It's both stifling and relentless, this pursuit of perfection. It's stifling because we fear not doing it right or getting it wrong, so we avoid doing anything at all: we delay starting. It's relentless because we fear that what we do is not good enough, so we avoid sharing anything at all: we delay finishing. Delay, delay, delay, all to mask our fear of being imperfect.

Perfection can be trying. It can be hard to endure and impossible to reach, but it can also stop us from making an effort to do something, to try and fail. In the same way that perfectionism stalls progress in our daily lives, it stalls progress in our society. We cannot move forward, we cannot learn and unlearn, we cannot change if we are stifled to the point of inaction.

The trap of perfectionism is that it can be a self-fulfilling prophecy. We fear getting things wrong or not being good enough, but if we're not willing to encounter our own imperfections—if we don't open ourselves up to failure—we won't do anything. We can convince ourselves that perfectionism, like indecision, can be another cosy nook to nestle into—if you don't try doing the thing, then you never have to confront doing it imperfectly. But a life spent in a comfortable corner is hardly a life well lived.

Something is better done than forever suspended in perfection. To do anything, we must be willing to get it wrong, to be bad at something, to fall short of perfection. The only way out is through.

For the perfectionist, 'trying' isn't really in our vernacular. 'Trying' exposes where we might have gaps in our knowledge, and highlights a particular incompetency. *Why am I here, still trying, when I should be there?* 'Trying' can be judged a waste of time. *If it won't be perfect, why try?* But there is nothing shameful about trying—it's the not-trying that haunts us.

I'm reminded of a scene in the film version of *Animals*, adapted by the author of the novel, Emma Jane Unsworth. The creatively blocked protagonist, Laura, meets classical pianist Jim for a first date in a bookstore cafe. Surrounded by aspiring writers tapping away at their laptops, she comments on how she pities them, still here, still trying, still getting nowhere. 'How do you know they're getting nowhere?' Jim asks. As he points out, the very act of trying is a step towards getting somewhere.

Perhaps it's taking the imperfect steps that we want to avoid. Far more appealing to skip over the part where we are flailing, and land squarely at the point of success, recognition and perfection. Reflecting on the beginning of her writing career, Ashley C. Ford told me that she had trouble imagining herself as a writer. Like many of us, the voice in the back of her head took over: 'Who are you to be a writer? Who are you to tell stories about you or your life?' Such doubts stemmed in part from her perfectionism. 'I think I spent a lot of my life wanting to jump over progression straight into perfection,' she said.

We want to bypass the part of the process where we only get incrementally better at something, but wind up feeling deflated when we realise we can't skip over our own progress. As Ashley told me, 'It was crushing my self-esteem and really messing with my self-confidence, too.' Cut to Ashley's career as a speaker, podcaster, writer and author of *Somebody's Daughter*; when I asked what changed, she told me, 'I just got to a point where I was like, why be your own bully?'

Perfectionism fools us into thinking that we are striving for quality, when in reality we are being our own bully with taunts that we're not good enough or never will be so. Sometimes these come from external sources—from our parents or our fourth-grade schoolteachers, or societal messages that seep into our unconsciousness or create very real obstacles. But in pursuing perfection, we are chasing a shadow we will never quite catch up with. In the meantime, we turn what could be a joyful, self-exploratory experience into a battle with ourselves. There will never be headway without imperfection. To return to the first date scene in *Animals*: Laura has written ten pages of her novel in ten years, and hesitates to share so much as a scribbled note from her journal. If we don't allow ourselves to try to sit with the part where we aren't good enough, we don't get anything down on the proverbial page. We must embrace trying. As Jim flirtatiously reminds Laura in the cafe, 'I believe we are not defined by who we are, but how we try to be. So, leave them alone.'

To overcome perfectionism, we must learn to leave ourselves alone—to stop being our own bullies, stop judging ourselves for taking messy incremental steps, and instead focus on the act of trying. At some point, we must put perfectionism aside and try— and try repeatedly. As Jim says, 'I'm only a pianist because I sit and practice every day.'

When I'm caught in hesitation or putting something off, I try to remind myself that sometimes the only antidote to being afraid of the work is to do the work. We may delay trying because we're afraid we'll find something hard, or discover we lack talent, but the only way to get better is through the doing. The fear dissipates when we do the thing, as Garth Greenwell said in his 2019 Bennington College commencement speech: 'The only time the anxiety lessens is when I'm bent over my notebook doing the only work that matters: trying to write a decent sentence, then another decent sentence, then one good page and another.'

When we focus on getting better this way, we shift the emphasis from *perfecting* something to simply *trying* something. As the entrepreneur, author, TV presenter, podcaster and 'doer of things' Lillian 'Flex Mami' Ahenkan told me, 'I feel like for the most part, hesitation or insecurity comes from not trying—if you haven't tried it, it must be hard. The moment you put pen to paper or get the software and give it a whirl, you realise it's not that hard. Put your brain to work.' Through trying, we often discover something was worse in our head, and we only wish we tried sooner.

For some of us, imperfection gets in the way not of starting something but of finishing something. We may fear that something isn't good enough, that we've got it wrong or that we'll be criticised for our efforts, so we backtrack before the finish line. There will always be ways to improve a thing—so part of trying is also learning that done is better than perfect, so we can bring our learnings to the next thing. Trying may be the antidote to perfection, but it isn't without its own frustrations. Trying is something we have to sustain with perseverance, so we must be careful not to stymie our efforts by trying too hard. As the scholar Edward Slingerland argued in his book *Trying Not to Try*, sometimes the harder we try, the more elusive something becomes. Some things we strive to create for ourselves might be better pursued indirectly—such as happiness, character or joy. 'We too often devote ourselves to pushing harder or moving faster in areas of our life where effort and striving are, in fact, profoundly counterproductive,' he noted.

Slingerland pointed to the Chinese concept of *wu-wei*—which translates as 'no trying' or 'no action'—as a way of counteracting relentless trying or striving, but it is not to be confused with dull inaction. Rather, it's something more akin to a flow state or getting 'in the zone'. The effortlessness of something can make it feel as if we are doing nothing, even if we're creating a brilliant work of art or solving a complex problem.

This notion reminds me a lot of the backstory behind the poet Charles Bukowski's succinct epitaph on his tombstone: 'Don't try.' It's said to originate from a letter to John William Corrington, in which Bukowski recounted his response to being asked how he writes. Bukowski replied: 'You don't try. That's very important: "not" to try, either for Cadillacs, creation or immortality.' Instead, we wait. 'If nothing happens, you wait some more. It's like a bug high on the wall. You wait for it to come to you. When it gets close enough you reach out, slap out and kill it. Or if you like its looks you make a pet out of it.'

We can spend so much of our days chasing proverbial bugs on the wall, only for the things we want to flee from our grasp. Not trying isn't the same as giving up—it means having the patience to wait for what is truly for us, rather than pursuing something that is not. When something is for us, we still need to make an effort to do it, but it will be effortless in that we are no longer chasing it around the room. We can sit with it, make a pet out of it and find ourselves making a start.

We will make many mistakes

Behind the fear of imperfection, we often find the fear of making a mistake. We might stick to what we know to avoid getting something wrong, but in doing so we can become confined by our own perfectionism.

In her TED Talk on grit, Angela Duckworth described people who know how to succeed but not how to fail as 'fragile perfects'. This can be a cause for concern, she says. 'I worry about people who cruise through life, friction-free, for a long, long time before encountering their first real failure. They have so little practice falling and getting up again. They have so many reasons to stick with a fixed mindset. I see a lot of invisibly vulnerable high-achievers stumble in young adulthood and struggle to get up again.'

Perhaps it's no wonder many of us can relate to being a 'fragile perfect' when there is societal pressure to be just so—making a misstep might result in humiliation, both private and public. We observe the pile-on of criticism of other people when they falter, which only makes it harder to practise falling and getting up again. Better to never make a mistake, to never fall—better to stay in the safe confines of theoretical perfection.

Such insistence on being perfect—both internally and externally—means that many of us find it unbearable to be only so-so at something. This fear of mediocrity seeps into every part of our daily lives. As Tim Wu explored in his article 'In Praise of Mediocrity' for *The New York Times*, the reason many people put off the things they want to do is fear of being bad at them. 'We are intimidated by the expectation—itself a hallmark of our intensely public, performative age—that we must actually be skilled at what we do in our free time,' he notes. 'Our "hobbies", if that's even the word for them anymore, have become too serious, too demanding, too much an occasion to become anxious about whether you are really the person you claim to be.' As Wu points out, we no longer jog around the block, but train for a marathon; it's no longer passing a pleasant afternoon with watercolours and your water lilies—you are trying to land a gallery show, or at least garner a respectable social-media following.

When we rush to the end—to the stage where we are skilled professionals—without so much as trying our hand at something, we can quickly become disenchanted. As amateurs in disguise, we feel so far behind that we can't really learn anything from the process.

What we don't realise is that we don't need to be perfect at something—or for the result to be impressive—for it to be a worthwhile pursuit. In fact, it's when we are amateurs, flailing and imperfect, that we have the most to gain. Being a beginner means we have to be willing to ask stupid questions, to learn through making mistakes, to simply experiment and risk feeling humiliated.

There is more to gain from failing than from being perfect. When I interviewed Jeremy Wortsman, the director of the artists' agency The Jacky Winter Group, he mentioned that he plays ice hockey a couple of times a week, despite not being very good. 'Even though I've been playing my entire life, I'm still really bad. But I think it's amazing to keep doing something you are terrible at. Being humbled and wanting to get better at something is a really important challenge.'

It's important, I believe, to be humbled by our own humanness. In doing the thing we're not so great at, we face what we once feared—except instead of feeling humiliated in the eyes of others, we feel humbled in our own. The latter is the only viewpoint we really have—even when we're worrying about what other people think of us, we are really just worrying about what we *think*

I DIDN'T DO THE THING TODAY

they think. Perhaps we have a choice about whether to feel humiliated, or humbled and human. Maybe taking that clumsy pottery class every week can help us remember we are a messy, fallible, imperfect human who won't be the perfect parent, or perfect friend, or perfect activist—and neither will anyone else.

So how do we sidestep the societal pressure to be perfect and find the confidence to begin? Perhaps we start by releasing the idea that we'll feel confident and ready before we start. As the actor Hugh Laurie said in an interview with *TimeOut*, when asked what made him step up to making his own album of songs, 'It's a terrible thing, I think, in life to wait until you're ready. I have this feeling now that actually no one is ever ready to do anything. There is almost no such thing as ready. There is only now. And you may as well do it now. Generally speaking, now is as good a time as any.' We can fool ourselves into waiting for the perfect stretch of time, or the perfect environment, or the perfect set of tools before we begin something new. But it's a myth that we have to wait for a sign, or until we've acquired the right skill set. Confidence doesn't come from having the perfect desk space or the perfect tools—it comes through making mistakes and then trying again. We simply begin by being a beginner.

Many of us might struggle to stick at something because it's uncomfortable to be bad at something—or we might even quit because being in the messy middle causes so much frustration and despair. But it's important to recognise that almost everyone has no idea what they're doing. Confidence isn't an innate trait—it's something built through experience. Doing something we're bad at allows us to gain experience, and through such experiences we gain the confidence to do it again. We now have the knowledge it can be done, or at least some insight on how to do it better next time.

Building confidence isn't a simple, upward trajectory—we will continue to bump into self-doubt. We are our own worst critics, but perhaps for good reason—we know what we deem to be quality, and we know our skills or abilities aren't quite there yet. Self-doubt can remind us that we still have more to learn, and so be the very thing that propels us to gain more experience.

As a beginner, we can be the fool who rushes in. This provided us with the experience to finally see when we are being a fool. But then we continue to learn and grow, eventually to the point that we feel confident in our knowledge and experience—or that we have proven to ourselves that we can pick ourselves back up from failure. As my mother always says, the best thing to do when you miss a bus is catch another.

Perfectionism is an illusion, but if there were a path to it, it would be one of iteration. I'm reminded of my conversation with the street artist Rone. Working on large-scale murals, he admitted that the fear of making a mistake—a really big, nine-storey mistake in the middle of the city—brought a lot of mental pressure. The solution was to start small and be open to iteration. 'My approach was to start with smaller works, so I could remind myself that if it all goes wrong, I could just paint over it,' he said. 'As I became more confident, the works got bigger. Now when I do something that is irreversible, I know my limits so I can pull it off.'

What I took from this is that success is just a set of well-curated failures: a collection of smaller mistakes that we paint over and learn from, again and again, until our fear of being bad at something is replaced by the confidence that comes from experience. We will keep making new mistakes—and sometimes the same ones as we try and try again—but we can learn from them too.

On any given day, we might find ourselves tallying up all the little things that went wrong—the small slights, the awkward encounters, the ways we hurt people inadvertently, the criticisms we received, and the straight-up failures. But maybe we need to view the tally another way—not as errors to correct, but as tiny little lessons learned. The more mistakes we make, the more we learn about who we are. As the musician Kira Puru told me, 'Just make mistakes and learn to be comfortable with them, learn what you didn't like about them, learn who you are in them. Mistakes can really teach you a lot.'

We may begin to see our mistakes as a sign that we're trying—that we're accumulating enriching experiences, iterating and gaining confidence. As the proverb goes, if you don't make mistakes, you don't make anything. Though it's important to take note of our mistakes and learn from them, it's equally important not to wallow. As Bill Murray put it, 'I made a lot of mistakes and realized I had to let them go. Don't think about your errors or failures, otherwise, you'll never do a thing.'

We contain multitudes

Much of the time, I think our pursuit of perfection is really a pursuit of a better life—if we could have the perfect career, the perfect relationship, the perfect body, the perfect home, we might finally feel at ease.

But we are not perfect—we are contradictions. We are virtue and vice, strength and weakness. We are both kind and impatient, we are glorious and we are self-destructive, we are striving and we are disorganised. When I interviewed one creative couple, performer Frankie Valentine and musician Mojo Ruiz de Luzuriaga, known professionally as Mo'Ju, it was refreshing to see how our contradictions can merge. Mojo described herself as 'really disorganised and scatter-brained', and Frankie chimed in: 'I think the positive flipside to being disorganised is that you very much live in the present. That is why you have such interesting interactions and form such special relationships because you are not distracted by all the mundane stuff. Being disorganised is part of your creativity.'

In each of our perceived weaknesses, we will find a strength, and the opposite can also be true. Yet in the pursuit of perfection, we try to iron out our weaknesses, not realising we might not be who we are without them—they are equal parts of who we are.

As the artist and author Austin Kleon told me, we don't need to sand off our edges. 'We're so obsessed with life-hacking and with becoming these productive, shining examples of ourselves, but so much of good creative work comes from being a person that has tensions in their life.' For Austin, this means embracing his 'deeply lazy' side as well as his 'driven workaholic' side. 'For a long time, I thought I had to pick one side, but I've realised it's sometimes bouncing between these two modes that really gives my life meaning—I don't feel the work would be meaningful if I didn't have those deeply lazy moments, too.'

Each of us likely has our own particular set of contradictions and rough edges, which not only make us more interesting to one another, but also offer a counterpoint within ourselves. For me, there is overlap between my deep inclination to be impulsive, and my deep yearning for order and plans. The two qualities create a tension. I'm good at planning and drafting goals and making lists of everything I want to do, but then my whims have other ideas. My organised self—a perceived strength—never ceases to come up with things for me to do, and gets carried away with lofty goals. Then my whims remind me not to take on too much: to be more open to how the day unfolds. It sometimes feels like two steps forward and one step back (and sometimes sideways), but perhaps that's more realistic than a perfect, upward trajectory.

I'm learning to see that perhaps it's not about ironing out these tensions and attempting to become some perfect version of myself, but rather accepting what I already am—a far from perfect contradiction. Instead of constraining ourselves to a perfect square, we oscillate among our various contradictions, playing snakes and ladders as we move between our multitudes.

Our weaknesses and our strengths are not set in stone. We experience different tensions at different times. We are made up of countless opinions, promises, preferences that can morph depending on our particular viewpoint. As the poet Ralph Waldo Emerson said in the essay 'Self-Reliance', 'Speak what you think now in hard words, and to-morrow speak what to-morrow thinks in hard words again, though it contradicts everything you said today—to be great is to be misunderstood.'

We can become hesitant—stubborn, even—when it comes to changing our minds. But when we admit to our contradictions, to our weaknesses, to our imperfections, we can step into ourselves.

It's the tensions in our life that make it interesting, not the perfections. In fact, when we encounter perfection in others—or at least our subjective definition or perception of it—we tend to find it rather dull, perhaps even insufferable. We don't want to be spectators to someone's illusionary perfection—we want to connect with their flaws and be reassured that we aren't alone in our own.

We put so much effort into striving for perfection, but it's often the imperfections in others we are often most charmed by—so why don't we allow ourselves to be charmed by our own, too? When we let our imperfections see the light, we connect with others. I remember reading in *The Guardian* about the Princeton University professor Johannes Haushofer: when he published his 'CV of Failures' it was celebrated and replicated, showing just how much we crave transparency around failure, mistakes and imperfection. Behind the act of vulnerability was an attempt to 'balance the record' and encourage others to pick themselves back up in the face of failure.

When we open up about our mistakes and failures, we give other people permission to do the same. We become a little more flexible, a little more creative about how we can be in the world. We can embrace being the imperfect academic, the imperfect student, the imperfect friend, the imperfect parent, the imperfect business owner. We can embrace our tensions, even be wooed by them, rather than trying in vain to conceal them.

It's an ongoing process, navigating our tensions and getting to know our multitudes. But we can show up, show up, show up—imperfect and trying, rather than not at all.

At the End of
the Day

15

The Generosity of Kindness

Three things in human life are important:
The first is to be kind.
The second is to be kind.
And the third is to be kind.

Henry James, overheard by his nephew Billy James

Being creative with our days, being open to the ebb and flow, is about finding not just our own way of being in the world, but our way of being with each other. As the author Rebecca Solnit put it in a *Guardian* article, 'We Could Be Heroes: An Election-Year Letter', 'Every minute of every hour of every day you are making the world, just as you are making yourself, and you might as well do it with generosity and kindness and style.'

When we narrow our day to how productive we are, we leave little space for generosity and kindness. When we have a crowded day, a catch-up with a friend or a conversation with a neighbour might seem a burden. When we hide our imperfections, we can dampen our opportunity to connect. When we pursue higher, better, more, we may overlook those around us. We don't see each other, we don't hear each other, we don't extend enough kindness to each other when we are confined to the doing.

When I survey my days, I see that it's often kindness that refreshes them. When someone steps aside to let us pass, to help us pick up the contents of a spilled bag, to ask our name, to stop to help in a moment of crisis, to say thank you, to listen when we tell them how we are, to say that they love those cobalt-blue boots we're wearing, to turn and to smile a 'sorry' when we're impatiently waiting behind them, these kindnesses can shift our mood, soften our irritation with the day. We might even summon a smile in return.

A gesture of kindness from someone can scoop us out of a bad day, and buoy us for hours, even days, afterwards. Yet we can easily miss or dismiss these exchanges. What's a smile worth, anyway? Perhaps nothing, when viewed through our doing-obsessed lens— but through the lens of creativity, fleeting kindnesses can make us forget what we were so upset about and plant us back in our days so we can remember to be kind, too. We think we can't possibly make a difference to the world, but one kind encounter can pulsate through countless lives. When someone is kind to us, that action has the power to make not only our own day better, but the days of the people around us. That kind smile from a stranger can be the very reason you offer a listening ear to a friend later that same afternoon, making their day better in the process. Kindness begets kindness—softening and spreading, softening and spreading. As the ancient Greek tragedian Sophocles wrote in *Ajax*, 'Kindness it is that brings forth kindness always.'

In this way, kindness can remind us that we are connected. We can spend our days avoiding each other, independent, not needing anyone or anything else to support us. In an individualistic society, our self-sufficiency or self-made success is lionised, but we're never entirely self-sufficient or self-made—we are the composite of our connections to people, whether the link is obvious or hidden from view. We do need each other—giving help, and receiving it, is what shapes us. In our modern lives, we can get so caught up in whether we are making progress or being productive that we overlook that so much of the world we live in is about connecting—with our wants, with each other, and between things and places. As the academic and artist Tyson Yunkaporta told me, sustainability is about establishing strong connections: 'Your way of being is your way of relating, because all things only exist in relationship to other things. This is the work of your heart.'

It's the work of our heart to notice the connections and relationships we have to things we can't even grasp. I think being connected is different to being in company. It's how we relate, and how kind we are in the relating. In this way, I think we can be by ourselves but still connected to the many people around us, and be kind, loving, humane. We can have someone come into our life just for a moment, and our life can be completely changed, and vice versa. We can be challenged by the opinions of people we never meet. We can try not to keep someone else waiting for something. We can go without speaking to a certain person for months, or even years, but when we finally do talk again, it feels like home.

So perhaps there's something to be said for trying to be kinder than necessary, in order to deepen our connections to one another while we're here. After all, when we experience loneliness, it's often because of a lack of quality company, not a lack of company. It can be a comfort to focus on the quality rather than the quantity of our connections—it allows us to see that we can make various touchpoints in our days count. These touchpoints can be found in varied places: at our local coffee shop, at the gym, at work, at that pottery class, at the local park. They can also be in our exchanges— we can add dollops of kindness to deepen how we connect, we can experiment with paying someone a compliment each day, or we can store the compliments we receive, rather than holding on to the insults. We can connect when we share an anecdote from our day or even the news. We can bring a smile by adding a friendly note to our email signature. We can invite a friend along for an 'errand hang' instead of dashing around solo. We can focus on making someone's day brighter, instead of lamenting how our own is panning out.

There are times when our life is open: we let in more inter- actions, make more connections, go more places. At other times, we have a more closed life, where we deepen those connections— even if it's just our connection with ourself. We need to find ways to be kind to ourselves as well as others, after all, and perhaps this starts with how we connect to our own self and our own thoughts. The thing about our doing-obsessed society is that it can cause us to be so hard on ourselves: we ruminate on the fact that we didn't do the thing today, or we didn't do enough, or we aren't good enough. We think that to be better, we need to make some drastic life change, but perhaps we simply need to be a bit kinder to ourselves and allow for the moment we are in.

When we are present in this way with ourselves, people can sense it and are drawn to it—without us necessarily doing a thing. As the writer Caitlin Moran put it, 'Just resolve to shine, constantly and steadily, like a warm lamp in the corner, and people will want to move towards you in order to feel happy.' There's the thread of connection once more—even our kind thoughts can light up a room for others.

Perhaps there's a lesson there both for us and for those around us: what if, instead of fixating on what we did today, we made it a habit to offer kindness in all its forms to share the warmth? That would be an interesting twist on our obsession with improvement—the focus would be on being a better human, rather than always striving for better. It's not some hack, some improvement technique or optimising our days that will save us, but our connections. It's not just what we do that shapes us, but all that we are, all that we experience, all that we extend to others. Being kind to a stranger, offering encouragement rather than criticism or lending a listening ear may build our character more than our accolades, accomplishments or successes ever will.

The habit of being a little kinder than necessary may be the very thing that can untether us from our doing obsession. No longer is it simply about what we did or didn't do in a day, but also whether we extended our kindness in small but impactful ways to those we encountered, whether we felt affection for them or not. This is easier said than done, especially when it feels like the world is taking everything from us. Why should I smile at a stranger when they will probably ignore it? Do I really have to be kind to someone I dislike or disagree with? Must I really be bothered with being kind when I'm having such a bad day?

While many of us wouldn't like to think of ourselves as unkind, we often need to remember to be kind and generous as it easily slips from our focus. It can be exhausting, if we're honest, this being kind business. And it can even leave us feeling vulnerable, as often unkindness comes from a position of defence—of an opinion, a position, an identity. If we let down our defences, we fear someone will take advantage of us.

Kindness can also be low on our priority list in a world that's geared towards progress, growth, success. It can seem like it takes a lot of effort to extend kindness for no clear reward—there's no financial gain, no improved output, no obvious advantage.

But there are inherent rewards to be found in kindness. When you talk positively about someone, it does come back to you. When we're kind to someone, they're often kind in return. When we're happy to see someone, they're happy to see us. When something good happens to us and we share it, we share the good. When we can't find the light, we can reflect the light we see in others. When we're kind, we're softened, and we can see that often others are trying their best too.

At times, we might make all sorts of kind gestures but still assume the worst in others. Perhaps learning to be more generous in our assumptions of others is the kindest act of all. We can be quick to form snap judgements; we easily assume other people are simple, whereas we are complex. Another popular way to frame

I DIDN'T DO THE THING TODAY

this is that we judge others by their actions, and ourselves by our intentions. When someone else is late, for example, we take that action to mean they are disorganised, whereas when we're late, it's because of something outside our control. We find justifications for ourselves, but find it more difficult to do so for others if we are not practised. We can flip this tendency and instead try to judge people by their good intentions and hold our own actions to account. Whether it's someone who is late or who comes across as rude to us, it's in such instances that we should keep the principle known as Hanlon's razor in mind: 'Never attribute to malice that which is adequately explained by ignorance.'

When we are a little kinder than necessary and make generous assumptions, we see that often the actions of others, however rude or irritating, are not personal. We can remember to be kind to unkind people because they often need it the most. Often people aren't being unkind on purpose, but rather simply living their days too—encountering bumps, forgetting to be kind, just as we all do. That's why, if we can remember, we can be the ones to refresh someone's day. Softening and spreading, softening and spreading.

As well as being generous in our assumptions, we can be generous in our actions, our time and our resources. We might hesitate to be generous as it often requires a personal inconvenience, discomfort or even sacrifice. But perhaps that's simply a perception—maybe we have nothing to lose and everything to gain from our generosity because it's what enables connection.

When we see that we don't lose anything by giving, we can be generous without expecting anything in return. We can give more than we take in our days. Can you bring energy to the people around you, rather than drain it? Can you make someone else's day better, rather than worse? Can you listen more than you talk?

Such generosity doesn't have to be reserved for our inter-actions with people: we can also show it towards the planet and the communities of which we are part. Are you contributing to your local community? Are you helping where you can with what you have? Are you less impressed by things you witness, and more involved? There are bound to be times when we cause upset, of course, whether intentionally or not—but we can strive to give more and take less, to make generous assumptions and to be a little kinder than necessary. We won't always remember to be kind, but we should be sure to seize the moments when we do. Whether it's by delivering a compliment, or sending a nice text to a friend when you think of them, or taking care of a chore for someone else, or donating to charity—do it right when you have the thought to do so. We might delay doing the thing today, but don't delay kindness—do it before the moment passes.

After all, isn't it the people in our lives rather than the things that are of utmost importance? Perhaps that's one way we can all be day artists—we may not be able to shape our day entirely the way we might hope, but we can shape the way we love. As Vincent van Gogh wrote in a letter to his brother Theo in 1888, 'The more I think it over, the more I feel that there is nothing more truly artistic than to love people.'

People never forget those who were kind in the moments they needed it most. People may not remember what you did, what your job title was or what exactly you said—but they will remember how you made them feel. We remember who believed in us when they didn't have to, but also when people underestimate us. We never know when either will come back around. So why don't we all focus on being kind—on the ways we can love people and extend generosity—rather than on being busy, productive, clever, impressive or successful? Sometimes, our days don't have to be much more complicated than that.

16

The Depth of Curiosity

Curiosity killed the cat,
but satisfaction brought it back.

Proverb

To be kind, we must be curious. When we are curious about other people, about ourselves, about our experiences, we become kinder—we strip away impatience, we don't rush into assumptions, we listen for answers. Curiosity seeps past the judgements we make about other people to reveal hundreds of little threads of connections we might never have known were there. It's curiosity that bonds us—the recognition that other people are fumbling too, messing it up, trying their best.

But we can be so incurious in our days. We stick to our assumptions, we ask no questions, we stay in our defences. We avoid rather than acknowledge, we stay on autopilot, not really knowing the people around us, not really caring, not really opening ourselves up.

When someone extends their curiosity—their kindness—towards us, we feel it. They pay attention, they are interested in our day, they ask, 'How was that for you?' or 'What is it like to be you?' Curiosity opens us to loving each other a little more fully. We don't rush past the difficult conversations; we don't try to reduce experiences to neat little packages; we don't try to wrap everything up and move on quickly.

How can we get interested in one another again? It strikes me how unadventurous we can be when it comes to being inquisitive. We can find ourselves working our way down a checklist of questions, each catch-up a systematic ticking off of items: *how are you, how is work, how is your partner, how is dating, how are the kids, how is this, how is that* . . . Sometimes we're not even listening for an answer, we're just waiting to share our own experiences. We don't allow for space between a question and a response. We don't ask that follow-up question, and another, and another, the prompts that could produce something novel. Instead of asking the rote 'How are you?', I've started to ask 'What are your days looking like?' as a way of empowering people to share the difficult, the mundane, the interesting details of their lives, instead of returning a closed response of 'Not too bad'.

If there is a thread to creating and re-creating our days, to overturning the day's obstacles, to reconfiguring the pressure of doing that we place on them, it is curiosity. The strong desire to know or learn something can help us cultivate aliveness towards others and ourselves—it can help us discover. It's in the discomfort that we discover something real, something shared.

It's curiosity that allows us to find value in the difficult things. We need to notice our days before we can go about them differently, and then we need to be curious enough to keep inspecting the various facets of our lives—the experiences, the people, the difficult things, the thoughts that come to us at three in the morning.

Many of us have to work a bit harder to realise what we want. But it's in the working harder, more creatively, that our life becomes arguably more interesting. Our days may have more depth and experience than those of someone who didn't have to work hard at all. Of course, this isn't to say we would wish for difficult things, but it's curiosity that allows us to find value within them. As the composer John Cage wrote, 'Wherever we are, what we hear is mostly noise. When we ignore it, it disturbs us. When we listen to it, we find it fascinating.' Being curious is what reminds us to listen, to pick up something fascinating when we fall. Perhaps it's a lesson, a change in perspective, or at least something to hold on to during our lacklustre days. This act of seeing one experience slightly differently can be a doorway to seeing our entire lives differently.

To find something to be curious about—to learn something—can bring shimmer back to our days. As the novelist T.H. White wrote in *The Once and Future King*, 'The best thing for being sad is to learn something. That's the only thing that never fails.' I try to recall this advice when I'm navigating a difficult thing, or find myself in a lull. It's taken me to poetry classes, to new books, to just sitting and watching the world go by. Sometimes I'll even just make a list of things to learn to remind myself of all the curious possibilities in my days—a list of new ways forward.

Unlike striving for a particular outcome, learning never fails, because, like creativity, it expands. White continued: 'Learn why the world wags and what wags it. That is the only thing which the mind can never exhaust, never alienate, never fear or distrust, and never dream of regretting. Learning is the only thing for you. Look what a lot of things there are to learn.'

We all have a lot of things to learn—and they don't have to cost us a thing. We do not have to consume something new, we can learn something new. Being a learner doesn't have to mean enrolling in a steady stream of expensive courses—we can simply be a student of our days. We can learn from our conversations, our tensions, the problems we solve, our failures, our successes, the difficult things we endure, the risks we take. We can learn from growing older, from rejection, from our shortcomings, from our talents, from discovering new things. If you're not sure what it is you want to learn, look to the things you're afraid to do, or that you tell yourself you'd never do. Start there.

Learning puts us back in touch with doing things that are just for us or for the benefit of the people we love, and not because we want to impress others. It can be a rare gift we give ourselves when we learn something just for ourselves—that's learning driven by curiosity, not by our desire for success or status.

Coincidentally, when we take an interest in learning something, we become more available to life, and life becomes more interesting. Interest begets interest—when you become interested in things, more things become interesting to you. You look around, and what you see seems to multiply. As the artist Henri Matisse wrote in *Jazz*, 'There are always flowers for those who want to see them.' Most of the time, we can find something interesting in our day if we allow ourselves to see it instead of rushing past it, or becoming deflated by the dailiness of it all.

Being *interested* in the world around us and the people in it can propel, expand and nourish us—but it is also what makes us *interesting*. This interest can be directed at almost anything. To paraphrase a quote often attributed to Henry Miller, we can develop an interest in life as we see it around us—the people, things, literature, music. Our days are rich with things to be interested in if we're not so lost in ourselves. It's in the act of being extremely interested in something or doing things that are interesting to us that we light up for others and become more interesting to them. This is perhaps why we are drawn to experts, to artists, to musicians, to that person at the party who listens to our stories: they take whatever they are interested in extremely seriously, which can render the ordinary into the extraordinary. They're living in their days, and we can feel it.

The curiosity to learn, to be interested, to be kind is how we find the extraordinary in the ordinary. We so often overlook the ordinary, or want to rid it from our days. We multitask, we outsource, we turn to life hacks to avoid the mundane, we project a shimmering version of our lives to others. But behind the scenes, the ordinary will always remain—and it can be where we connect to our curiosity and wonder. As Hans Christian Andersen wrote, 'The whole world is a series of miracles, but we're so used to seeing them that we call them ordinary things.' Being curious about the ordinary means embracing the notion that we don't have to do something extraordinary right now—we don't have to think big. We can just do this ordinary thing, and do it well.

So what if we found a way to find the miracles in the ordinary, instead of trying to optimise the humdrum to the point of its elimination? After all, without the ordinary, we'd be missing where life happens. As Mike Powell wrote in 'Letter of Recommendation: Washing Dishes' for *The New York Times*, 'Most of life is ordinary; that ordinary isn't the enemy but instead something nourishing and unavoidable, the bedrock upon which the rest of experience ebbs and flows.'

Indeed, the ordinary is the bedrock for the creativity we want to bring to our days. When our day feels broken, misaligned or lacklustre, it's creativity that might allow us to devise ways to mend it, or to work with what we have—and it's curiosity that propels us to lean into the cracks. If creativity can expand our days, curiosity can deepen them: it shows us who we are by allowing us to get closer to ourselves.

As we have seen, we only change and discover new ways forward by inspecting what may cause us guilt, shame or anxiety—not covering them over by doing more, but by doing them differently, or learning to embrace ourselves as we are. In this way, curiosity is the key to creativity—our human creativity. It's what helps us to renew, to move through periods of transition or dullness, and to change.

It's through curiosity that we can connect to the parts of ourselves that live behind the cracks we find in our days. We can be curious about the wants that lie behind our expectations, and about what fulfils us rather than how we fill time. We can find the strength in our weaknesses, the delight behind the discipline, the surprise when we put a plan aside.

Curiosity is what allows us to see that the most ordinary fact about our lives is already rather extraordinary—we're here. We're living. We may not be sure why, but we're going about our days anyway, and that's rather remarkable.

In our doing-obsessed culture, we tend to focus on those things we can measure, but some of the most important things in life simply can't be measured. Instead of orientating our days towards getting ahead and striving to become someone extraordinary, we can find the extraordinary in our own ordinary life. We can walk on the side of the street where the sun is shining. We can eat a raspberry and remember what a wonder a raspberry is. We can love someone or something and notice that love expand. We can admire that person's hat. We can take inspiration from the lives of others to bring a spark to our own. We can marvel at how the glass casts a rainbow on the train floor as we commute home.

It's the ordinary things in our days that can help us find delight, satisfaction and enjoyment if we learn to look. When we do this, regularly and often, we are cultivating a practice of being more curious and orientated to finding the beauty in ordinary things— interest begets interest, remember.

We don't need to change our days; we simply need to be curious about the ordinary things within them that might make them shimmer. As the author Rainbow Rowell wrote in *Attachments*, 'So, what if, instead of thinking about solving your whole life, you just think about adding additional good things. One at a time. Just let your pile of good things grow.'

I DIDN'T DO THE THING TODAY

Trying to solve our entire lives or comprehend the magnitude of circumstances and injustices outside our control can be overwhelming. But often there is a small good thing we can do to help ourselves and others. When our days have been upended and narrowed, to varying degrees and in varying ways, when we feel restless, uncertain or disheartened, this notion of adding good things, just one at a time, can be a comfort. What we can control is often small—the books we read, the thoughts we think, the people we spend time with, the kindness we extend to strangers, the things we pay attention to—but they are ordinary wonders.

It's often the bumps with the small, good, ordinary things that bring us extra-alive. So often I catch myself wanting more, but then I'll encounter something ordinary and good, and suddenly it all feels like enough—it's miraculous just to be going about this day. As the activist Rachel Cargle tweeted, 'Today I moved my body, I read, I wrote, I ate something green, I finished a whole bottle of water, I laughed, I prepped something, I completed something, I said I love you, I honoured a personal boundary and I breathed deeply. A good day.'

A good day doesn't have to be an optimised day; it can be rather simple. We can take note of the moments we feel extra-alive to build a repository of small, good, ordinary things that remind us life is extraordinary—what we're eating, who we're spending time with, what we're listening to, what place we're in, what we're doing. And we can keep adding to the list and re-creating it.

I decided to make my own list of small, good, ordinary things— journalling, chopping vegetables, sleeping on fresh sheets, tidying my desk, reading, tweezing my eyebrows, listening to a favourite song, making carbonara at midnight after a fun night out, calling a friend, sitting on a park bench, taking a sip of a dirty gin martini, holding hands, putting on a podcast, taking a nap, taking a walk, pleasuring myself, making a delicious wrap for lunch, sending a complimentary email to someone I think is doing a good job. It's a comfort to know that we don't have to overhaul our lives to find glimpses of satisfaction or happiness—we can simply pull something from our list of small, good, ordinary things and begin.

In fact, these small moments that we can control can also cultivate happiness—however we might define that—especially amid uncertainty. Dr Laurie R. Santos is the creator of the most popular course in the history of Yale University, 'The Science of Well-Being', which shows students how to live more fulfilling lives. By studying human happiness, she found it's not the big things like money and success that make us happy, but rather the simple, small things. As she said in a conversation with *The New York Times*, 'One of the most shocking [discoveries] for me was a study looking at how simple interactions with strangers positively affect your well-being. A simple chat with a stranger can make people feel great.'

These small, good, ordinary things can shape a day into something good, even amid a string of not-so-good days. They are the things we can do just for us—not for a badge of honour, not as a favour or to prove something. When they pile up, we slowly begin to have something we can stand on, things we have some control over, ballast that can steady us in our days.

So instead of trying to solve your whole life right now, cultivate your curiosity and try approaching things day by day; hour by hour; small, good, ordinary thing by small, good, ordinary thing. We don't know what the future holds, but if we can let a pile of small, good, ordinary things grow, we will create a bedrock for our days. This is what will help us be steady for the big things, too—for developing a better understanding of others, and of what we really want from our days, not just what we do in them. When we count the small, good, ordinary things in our days, it helps us realise that there will always be more to discover. That's the thing about being curious in our days—there's always something around the corner and we don't know what it's going to be. We take for granted that things can change in an instant. Most things will be okay, but not everything will be. Not everything a day brings is positive, but even on the days that something blindsides us, we can find some good— or remember that something good will come again. As the iconic Australian fashion designer and artist Jenny Kee told me, 'There are always surprises in your life, and for me, the highlight is always coming. What is it going to be? That's the mystery of life.'

Tomorrow is not just a new day, it's a different day—and if we're interested, if we're curious, we can look for the highlight within it, even if it's just one small, good, ordinary thing.

17

The Moments of Enjoyment

There are two things to aim at in life: first, to get what you want; and, after that, to enjoy it. Only the wisest of mankind achieve the second.

Logan Pearsall Smith, *Afterthoughts*

There will be *days like these*—and yet these are the days we all live in. Like the familiar bars of a daytime television theme song, our days can blend into the background of the living rooms of our lives; sometimes static, sometimes too loud, sometimes repetitive. I've often lamented how commonplace a day can be, how dull, how predictable. I've wished for a way to change the channel, or felt like I'm in a commercial break waiting for the real show to begin, only to be left wondering, *Is that all there is?*

But this is the real show—the *days like these* are the days of our lives. We're not on the way to a better life, we are in the middle of our lives—here, waiting for the bus, renovating the kitchen, patiently listening to our neighbour tell us about their sick cat, in the living room with the television on too loud.

We are never going to reach a point where our days are without drama, without friction, without cracks. Our days won't someday be smoothed over, full of ecstasy and elation—or perhaps completely calm and serene, if that's more your thing. There will always be stumbles, and we may as well navigate the day with them because that's the only way we can fully step into our lives.

Otherwise, what are we waiting for? We cannot wait until we're perfect, until we've got through our to-do list, until we've streamlined our routine, until we've fulfilled all our goals, ambitions and dreams—our real life is unfolding now. Perhaps that's our task as day artists—to strive to realise that each day is a little life, to remember that this very day is not a dress rehearsal, or to cultivate a small part of us that does. As the character Emily asks in Thornton Wilder's play *Our Town*, 'Do any human beings ever realize life while they live it?—every, every minute?' The stage manager replies, 'No. Saints and poets maybe . . . they do some.'

There is a fine line, I think, between ensuring that we don't coast through our days or postpone our lives, but also that we don't berate ourselves over how they unfold. It's not every day that we turn our lives around, that we do the thing. We must remember that life is often long enough to be patient with the time worthwhile things take, but it is also short, and we can start now. Like saints and poets, as day artists we can find some moments of the day in which we 'realize life' while we live it.

We can get caught in the slush of the day, deeming it either good or bad, successful or unsuccessful, productive or distracted, and forget to be present within it. Of course, we're only human—we can't expect to always be living right in the present, with no thoughts of yesterday or tomorrow. We don't always live in the moment, but we can take care of the moments by noticing them, by not taking them for granted, by not diminishing them. How we spend our days is how we slowly figure out how to spend our lives—when thought of in this way, it all counts. We are here just for a moment, so let's not fritter that time away with harsh judgements about what we did or didn't do. Instead, let's reflect on the moments we enjoyed—whether for the challenge, rest or pleasure they provided. It's moments, after all, that we can seize—and even then it's only some.

We've commonly mistaken the meaning of the Latin idiom 'carpe diem'—it's not to 'seize' the day, but rather to 'pluck' the day. If we return to the image of our days as fecund gardens, then in order to pluck the day we first need to survey what is blossoming, what is ripe, what is ready to harvest. This looks different from day to day, and season to season. We do not wish to dig it all up in a frenzy, but we should be careful in our selection, gently tending to a moment, careful not to crush or damage its stem or bruise the fruits of the day.

In each day, even *days like these*, there is something for us to pick—something we can pop in a vase on the windowsill and enjoy. So you didn't accomplish everything today. Maybe you didn't accomplish anything at all. But is it really a wasted day? There are myriad things to select from the garden of the day—sometimes novel, sometimes difficult, sometimes ordinary. If we're curious, if we're kind, we can always find something to enjoy.

I DIDN'T DO THE THING TODAY

We might overlook the moments within reach because we're waiting for something more significant to arrive, but the best way to make the most of our moments is to tend to them, to pick what we have in front of us. Maybe it's a private moment with ourselves, maybe it's time with our favourite person. Maybe it's a funny thing we remember that makes us laugh in public. Maybe it's that moment of boredom when an idea comes to us. These small moments are the significant moments. As the writer Robert Brault said, 'Enjoy the little things in life, for one day you may look back and realise they were the big things.'

Even when we can't find a moment to pick, maybe we can look back on our day as if we're returning after our death. The words of the late Amy Krouse Rosenthal, in *Encyclopedia of an Ordinary Life*, always come to me when I'm feeling not quite in the day:

> When I am feeling dreary, annoyed and generally un-impressed by life, I imagine what it would be like to come back to this world for just a day after having been dead. I imagine how sentimental I would feel about the very things I once found stupid, hateful or mundane. Oh, there's a light switch! I haven't seen a light switch in so long! I didn't realize how much I missed light switches! Oh! Oh! And look—the stairs up to our front porch are still completely cracked! Hello cracks! Let me get a good look at you. And there's my neighbour, standing there, fantas-tically alive, just the same, still punctuating her sentences with you know what I'm saying? Why did that bother me? It's so . . . endearing.

Maybe we can't expect to enjoy every day, but we can find it endearing. When we reach the end of the day, instead of berating ourselves for what we did or didn't do, we can be charmed by the ordinary moments of living and what our days can bring. As the writer Marieke Hardy told me, 'In my work life, social life and emotional life, I've always got something to look forward to—and sometimes that's a doughnut.' Imagine what someone would do with just a few days of your life, if they had the chance. Would they reserve their enjoyment in anticipation of the big things, or would they see that there's something to look forward to in something as simple as a doughnut? Would they worry about what they did or didn't do, or would they search for the moments they enjoyed? Would they notice what they have? Would they say what they want to say? Would they dance around in the fecund garden of the day? *Imagine just a few days of it.* What we all have in common is that each of us has had more than just a few days of this life. Yet we sometimes feel bored by it, disconnected, guilty that we're not doing it right, or that we don't deserve the special privileges we enjoy, on top of this shared privilege of life.

Perhaps the best thing to do with the privilege of living is to see it clearly—to see how precious it is, and not wallow in guilt or cause harm to others. The same can be said for our varying privileges: do not waste what you have. We cannot control how respected, accomplished and desired we are, or what will become of our days—or when an end to them will come. All we can do is enjoy the experience, learn how to treat special things, and resist conflating our productivity with our worth. That's how we can get the good out of every bit of it.

Just as no two of us are the same, neither are our days and the moments within them. Embrace them as they are, and as you are. After all, the most meaningful lives, I've learned, are often not the extraordinary, the perfect or the problem-free ones—they're the ordinary ones lived with creativity, curiosity, kindness and joy. Maybe that's all we really need to do today, to find something to value within. Something to be curious about, something to love, something to learn. That something might just be everything.

Even if you didn't do the thing today, find something to enjoy

- Enjoy the failures and mistakes—they're a sign we're trying.

- Enjoy the unknown—it's where we discover something new.

- Enjoy the rest, the boredom, the empty moments—that's where we find insight.

- Enjoy the busy, too—that's where we can find momentum.

- Enjoy the rut—that's where we can discover a new path.

- Enjoy the wobble—that's where we find the variances that light us up.

- Enjoy the learning—it's where we can never fail.

- Enjoy the limitations—it's where we find awe and creativity.

- Enjoy the choices we make as well as the plans that change— they're often the making of our lives.

- Enjoy the comparisons with another—it's where we find our secret joy.

- Enjoy the questions—because life would be dreary if we had all the answers.

- Enjoy the process—because the joy is in the doing, not the done.

- Enjoy the incomplete—because that means there's more to come.

- Enjoy the moments—if we tend to them, if we get the good out of every bit of them, what a life we'll have created.

I didn't do the thing today.
I didn't lament how the hours unfolded.
I didn't worry about wasted time.
I didn't allow my expectations to spoil what I have.
I didn't compare myself to others.
I didn't dwell in the undone.
I didn't strive; I didn't try to be perfect.
And it mattered. Because in all that I didn't do
I found my own measure of a day.

Acknowledgements

To my agent, Georgia Frances King, thank you for your unwavering encouragement and for being an expert guide through the book galaxy. To the wonderful team at Murdoch Books and collaborators: Corinne Roberts, for nudging this book along through its many iterations; Julian Welch, for your thoughtful suggestions and gentle fingerprint on my words; Evi O, for bringing your talent and creativity to the striking cover; and Julie Mazur Tribe, Vivien Valk, Sarah Hatton and the many other talented folk involved in bringing these pages to life, for your enthusiasm, patience and dedication.

To the many people across my life who have offered lessons about the things that matter. To my parents and family, for your love and encouragement, and for teaching me what it means to show up. Particularly to my mother, for your listening ears and for demonstrating the importance of being a life-long learner, and to my brother Nelson, for always knowing the nugget of wisdom that's needed for the different spirals one can encounter in a day.

To my delightful friends—old and new, fleeting and forever. You are daffodils in the fecund garden of my days, and have taught me to try new things, do fun things and appreciate small things. Particularly to those who kept me company during the writing process: Georgia O'Connor, for the countless virtual 'puddles', superb metaphors and smattering of 'I believe in yous'—you've taught me to poke life with a stick and make it dance, even (and perhaps especially) when life isn't being particularly fair. Anton De Ionno, for the best writing-filled days, for countless overstuffed lunchtime wraps and for evenings spent staying up too late talk-talk-talking— thank you for catching epiphanies and reminding me you've gotta enjoy life! Bethany Simons, for many virtual writing sessions, for your uncanny ability to find poetry in the everyday and for teaching me what it means to be true, flourishing and free. Jessica Wainwright, for being the sunniest deadline cheerleader and for reminding me of the quiet power of asking open-hearted questions and taking note of the details. Mari Andrew, for peppering my days with your brilliance and your encyclopaedic knowledge of feelings, and for the joy you share in dissecting the everyday—you teach us all how to sparkle. Anu Hasbold, for believing in my dreams since always, and for teaching me that while expectations may lead to disappointment, it's the unexpected joys we encounter that are worth cherishing.

To Frances Haysey, for the perfect writing nook and for being a brilliant sounding board. Jeffrey Phillips, for your unparalleled enthusiasm for creative ideas and for your generosity with your myriad talents. Julia Pelosi-Thorpe, for sharing your love of words with me and teaching me the Latin root of the word 'delight' and many others. Amelia Goss, for your impeccable eye and for many cherished flops on the couch. Eddie Harran, for being a wonderful 'gentle time' thesaurus and comparison companion. Spencer Harrison, for the kind prod I needed to start *Extraordinary Routines* all those years ago, and for reminding me that done is better than perfect.

To the many inspiring people whom I had the pleasure of interviewing for *Extraordinary Routines* and *Routines & Ruts*: for your time, for your pearls of wisdom and for your generous sharing of important things with the world—you've taught me and my dear readers and listeners that there are many ways to live our days.

To various things that accompanied the writing process: my desk bell, for sounding the perfect ding; Milanote, for being the ideal tool to organise my ideas, notes and the inner workings of my brain; and 'Ambient Chopin' by Peter M. Murray, for being almost 23 minutes long and the single song I listened to while writing.

This book was written on the stolen land of the Wurundjeri People of the Kulin Nation. I pay my respects to Elders past, present and emerging, and recognise their continuing culture and deep understanding of connection, creativity and curiosity.

For a list of favourite findings and things that informed this book, please visit madeleinedore.com/favourite-things.

Credits

Page 18: Quote from Toni Morrison courtesy of Wellesley College Archives, Library & Technology Services and ICM Partners.

Page 29: Quote from Annie Dillard reprinted by the permission of Russell & Volkening as agents for Annie Dillard, copyright © 1989 *The Writing Life* by Annie Dillard.

Page 171: Quote from Sylvia Plath reprinted by the permission of Faber and Faber Ltd as publishers of *The Unabridged Journals of Sylvia Plath* by Sylvia Plath.

Page 263: 'Returning to life after being dead' from *Encyclopedia of an Ordinary Life* by Amy Krouse Rosenthal, copyright © 2005 by Amy Krouse Rosenthal. Used by permission of Crown Books, an imprint of Random House, a division of Penguin Random House LLC. All rights reserved.

Index